Cataloguing Without Tears

D1196826

CHANDOS
INFORMATION PROFESSIONAL SERIES

Series Editor: Ruth Rikowski
(email: rikowski@tiscali.co.uk)

Chandos' new series of books are aimed at the busy information professional. They have been specially commissioned to provide the reader with an authoritative view of current thinking. They are designed to provide easy-to-read and (most importantly) practical coverage of topics that are of interest to librarians and other information professionals. If you would like a full listing of current and forthcoming titles, please visit our web site **www.library-chandospublishing.com** or contact Hannah Grace-Williams on email info@chandospublishing.com or telephone number +44 (0) 1865 884447.

New authors: we are always pleased to receive ideas for new titles; if you would like to write a book for Chandos, please contact Dr Glyn Jones on email gjones@chandospublishing.com or telephone number +44 (0) 1865 884447.

Bulk orders: some organisations buy a number of copies of our books. If you are interested in doing this, we would be pleased to discuss a discount. Please contact Hannah Grace-Williams on email info@chandospublishing.com or telephone number +44 (0) 1865 884447.

Cataloguing Without Tears

Managing knowledge in the information society

JANE M. READ

WITH CARTOONS BY ADRIAN CZAJKOWSKI

Chandos Publishing

Oxford · England · New Hampshire · USA

Chandos Publishing (Oxford) Limited
Chandos House
5 & 6 Steadys Lane
Stanton Harcourt
Oxford OX29 5RL
UK
Tel: +44 (0) 1865 884447 Fax: +44 (0) 1865 884448
Email: info@chandospublishing.com
www.library-chandospublishing.com

Chandos Publishing USA
3 Front Street, Suite 331
PO Box 338
Rollinsford, NH 03869
USA
Tel: 603 749 9171 Fax: 603 749 6155
Email: BizBks@aol.com

First published in Great Britain in 2003

ISBN:
1 84334 043 7 (paperback)

British Library Cataloguing-in-Publication Data.
A catalogue record for this book is available from the British Library.

The Publishers make no representation, express or implied, with regard to the accuracy of the information contained in this publication and cannot accept any legal responsibility or liability for any errors or omissions.

The material contained in this publication constitutes general guidelines only and does not represent to be advice on any particular matter. No reader or purchaser should act on the basis of material contained in this publication without first taking professional advice appropriate to their particular circumstances.

Typeset by Monolith – www.monolith.uk.com
Printed in the UK and USA

To my husband, Bill

Contents

Introduction   *ix*

Acknowledgements   *xv*

List of abbreviations   *xvii*

About the author   *xxi*

Part 1 The big picture

1   Why bother to catalogue?   **3**

What the catalogue is for   5

Anticipating the needs of users   10

Convincing your boss that cataloguing is important   12

2   What to catalogue?   **19**

What a catalogue record contains   20

Carved in stone? Writing a cataloguing policy for
your organisation   32

Into the abyss: the politics of cataloguing   37

3   Who should catalogue?   **43**

The process of cataloguing   44

How long does it take to catalogue a document?   48

Appropriate levels of staffing   51

Organising time   53

4   How to catalogue … and not reinvent the wheel   **57**

Choosing a records management system   59

International cataloguing standards   66

Subject cataloguing 91

Authority control 97

Part 2 The nitty-gritty

5 Is it a book, is it a journal …? 109

Distinguishing between formats 111

The awkward squad: loose-leaf files, websites and skeletons 127

6 What's a strange attractor? Cataloguing subjects you know nothing about 137

Finding the right subject headings 141

Verifying your information 148

Assigning subject and genre headings to fiction 150

7 *Ici on ne lit pas le français*: unknown languages and how to deal with them 153

What language is it? 158

Transcribing non-Roman writing systems 160

Understanding the subject 163

Parallel texts, multilingual footnotes and other excitements 167

Practical problems 169

8 Special cases 175

Manuscripts, archival collections and rare books 175

Graphic materials: pictures, postcards, book illustrations … 204

Children's books and related materials 209

Electronic resources 215

Appendix: Resources for cataloguers 219

Bibliography 227

Index 231

Introduction

So, you have become a cataloguer. Congratulations! Or maybe you have just become a metadata engineer. Congratulations again – you could equally well be called a cataloguer, because your job is essentially the same.[1] Your new job is challenging, intellectually demanding and absolutely vital to the operation of your information service. Or, in other words, you are the one who provides clues (in the form of catalogue records) which enable your colleagues and your clients to find the information they need quickly and efficiently.

That's the upside of the job. The downside is that cataloguing can often be boring and repetitive. Positive feedback from users of the catalogue is rare. Finally, cataloguers are regarded as nerdy even by other librarians. This, despite the fact that in the so-called 'knowledge economy' it is more important than ever before to have documents and other information resources accurately described with appropriate subject terms. Otherwise the famous aphorism about the Internet will come true in your organisation: 'The truth is out there... but I'm damned if I can find it.'

The purpose of this book is to provide an introduction to descriptive and subject cataloguing (but not classification) for librarians and other information professionals. It is arranged in two main parts. Part 1, *The big picture*, relates the theory of cataloguing to the practice of defining a cataloguing policy for your organisation, selecting suitable staff and choosing a cataloguing standard. Part 2, *The nitty-gritty*, considers some of the specific problems which you are likely to encounter as a cataloguer. An appendix follows which consists of a select list of resources for cataloguers.

Many great experts have written on the subject of knowledge management and how it differs from information management. The problem is that they don't agree among themselves:

> Information is not a synonym for knowledge, which is an intellectual concept, referring to the condition of knowing or understanding something ... Information and knowledge can be seen as closely related and complementary stages along the same road ... (Webb, 1998)

> ...information has no value, ie does not become knowledge, until it is used... (Ryan, 1999)

Personally, I would agree (up to a point) with the first writer and disagree violently with the second, but a debate on exactly what is meant by knowledge management and how it differs from information management, though interesting, does not help with the practical problem of how best to describe the materials in your library on the database so that library users can find what they want quickly and efficiently. So don't worry too much about whether you are cataloguing knowledge or information – concentrate on relatively easy questions such as what the title is and who published it.

In writing this book, I have tried to avoid jargon as much as possible but there are times when it is easier to use the correct (subject-specific) word to describe something than to provide a laborious explanation in plain English. Also, if you want other people to believe that you know what you are talking about it is sometimes important to use the buzzwords they are used to, so you need to learn them. Most of the jargon in this book may be found in Chapters 4, 5 and 8; I will be explaining it as I go along.

While we're on the subject of jargon, you will notice as you read through the text that I rarely use the word 'book' to describe things which you might be cataloguing. The reason for this coyness is that books are only one of many different formats you may encounter in your career. I usually use the word 'document' to denote books, journals, pamphlets, videos, pictures, computer files, web pages, audio tapes, manuscripts... 'Document' is not really an ideal term, because it implies a printed or written text to most people, but it's a little less vague than the other words in current use: 'resource' (popular among metadata engineers) and 'work' (as used in the International Standard for Bibliographic Description). I have also chosen to refer to your job as 'cataloguing' rather than 'metadata engineering', mainly because most people have some idea of what a catalogue is (and therefore what a cataloguer does) but need to have 'metadata' and 'metadata engineer' explained. Also, although it would be semantically correct to describe all cataloguers as metadata engineers (metadata just means data about data, so all library catalogues are sets of metadata) in practice the term is mainly used by those working on electronic resources such as websites and e-journals.

What you catalogue and how you catalogue it will depend to a large extent on who your library is intended to serve, and to a lesser extent on who is available to do the work and how much time they have to do it in. You could be working on your own in a small corporate library or with a team of several people in an academic library; you could be the only specialist cataloguer on the staff of a public library, or a cog in the cataloguing department of a national library. Your work might consist of cataloguing only items on one subject or in one language, or you might be expected to catalogue anything and everything acquired by your library, from books and journals to electronic documents and cuddly toys. You might have other tasks besides cataloguing to fit into your working day. One day, perhaps you could aspire to being a head cataloguer, in charge of a large department of cataloguing professionals and responsible for maintaining a huge database to internationally accepted standards, or even rise to the dizzy heights of being one of the people who writes international standards!

Cataloguers work in many different environments and create many different kinds of catalogue. I have therefore assumed that:

- you are creating records for an online public access catalogue (OPAC) or computer database;

- you are working in a library or information centre which includes at least some physical documents, as opposed to a virtual library which only has online resources.

I have not assumed that:

- you are using the Anglo-American Cataloguing Rules (AACR);
- you are encoding it on the computer according to the MARC (Machine-Readable Cataloguing) standard.[2]

Reading a book about cataloguing is not the best way to learn about it. The very best way to learn is to catalogue a wide variety of different materials with an experienced cataloguer at your elbow telling you what to do next (and why), but this is only feasible if you work in a large organisation with a cataloguing department consisting of more than one person. If you don't, you will have to sit down with the cataloguing guidelines for your organisation, put an icepack on your head and try to work it out for yourself. The (modest) aim of this book is to guide you through what to look for and how to get started. *Bon courage!*

Notes

1. Don't tell your boss if it's likely to have a negative effect on your pay packet!
2. There is a large selection of works available to help you with AACR and MARC; some of them are listed in the appendix at the back of the book.

Acknowledgements

I'd like to thank the following for their assistance:

- Adrian Czajkowski – without whose cartoons this book would have been a lot duller;
- Bill Read – for taking the photos, editing the image files, drawing the diagrams and generally being wonderful;
- Reading University Library – for granting permission to use photographs of items from their collections; and finally
- Chandos Publishing for commissioning the book!

Photographs used by permission:

- *Degrees of Fear* copyright to Sarob Press;
- *Drum and IBC Guide* copyright to Intapress Publishing;
- *A study of volatile precursors for the growth of cadmium sulphide and cadmium selenide* copyright to Michael Beer.

List of abbreviations

AACR	Anglo-American Cataloguing Rules
AAT	Art and Architecture Thesaurus (Getty Research Institute)
ACRL	Association of College and Research Libraries (US)
AV	audio-visual
BL	British Library
BT	broader terms
BUBL	BUBL Information Service (formerly Bulletin Board for Libraries, online)
CILIP	Chartered Institute of Librarians and Information Professionals
DC	Dublin Core
DCRB	*Descriptive Cataloguing of Rare Books* (Library of Congress, online)
EAD	Encoded Archival Description
GMD	graphic material designation
HTML	hypertext mark-up language
IFLA	International Federation of Library Associations and Institutions
ISAAR	International Standard Archival Authority Record for Corporate Bodies, Persons and Families

ISAD(G)	General International Standard Archival Description
ISBD	International Standard for Bibliographic Description
ISBD(A)	International Standard for Bibliographic Description of Antiquarian Books
ISBD(E)	International Standard for Bibliographic Description of Electronic Documents
ISBD(G)	General International Standard for Bibliographic Description
ISBN	International Standard Book Number
ISSN	International Standard Serial Number
KM	knowledge management
LCSH	Library of Congress Subject Headings
LP	long-playing (vinyl record)
MARC	Machine-Readable Cataloguing
MeSH	Medical Subject Headings (US National Library of Medicine)
NCA	National Council on Archives
NT	narrower terms
OCLC	Online Computer Library Center
ONIX	Online Information Exchange
OPAC	online public access catalogue
PC	personal computer
PDF	portable document format
RSLP	Research Support Libraries Programme
RT	related terms

SCAN	Scottish Archive Network
SGML	standard generalised mark-up language
TGN	Thesaurus of Geographical Names (Getty Research Institute)
UKOLN	UK Office for Library and Information Networking
ULAN	Union List of Artists' Names (Getty Research Institute)
URL	universal resource locator
XML	Extensible Markup Language

About the author

Jane Read was brought up in Cumbria (famous for its lakes), a confirmed book addict from an early age despite the fact that none of the rest of her family were. Graduating from York (famous for its minster) in 1986 with a BA in language and linguistic science, Jane made a brief foray into Essex to teach and then compounded the error by moving to Reading (famous for its gasworks) in 1989. In 2003 she finally came to her senses and returned to York.

Jane has 14 years' experience in academic libraries, mostly gained working for Reading University Library in a wide variety of roles, including project management, information desk work and cataloguing. Her most recent job title was Rare Books Cataloguer, which is both more and less exciting than you might think. She has contributed articles to professional journals such as *Library Technology* and *Catalogue & Index*, and spoke at the (CILIP) Rare Books Group's 2002 conference on children's books, contributing a paper on the cataloguing of rare children's books.

When not cataloguing, Jane enjoys singing, collecting early twentieth-century children's books and writing ghost stories.

The author may be contacted via the publishers.

Part 1

The big picture

Why bother to catalogue?

...a real three-cornered fight was just getting underway when Mrs Fosdyke, whom everyone had been ignoring, suddenly let out a wild shriek ...

They all turned. She was standing in the doorway of the pantry looking pale and distraught. In each hand she held a tin without a label.

'There's thousands of them!' she shrieked. 'And tops off packets and holes in the sides of things!'

Helen Cresswell, *Absolute Zero*

Given a choice between a number of different tasks, most information professionals would probably put cataloguing at the bottom of their list of priorities. It's a routine job. It can be boring. The rewards are neither immediate nor obvious. All of these make it an unattractive proposition by comparison with answering reference inquiries or updating the library website, except to those rare people who enjoy intellectual challenges for their own sake and do not mind taking pains over details which seem petty to the casual observer.

Yet cataloguing is more important than ever in the information world. It's easy enough to keep track of what is in a small collection of uncatalogued objects or documents, especially if you have personally used or read them. It is less easy when you have to manage a very large collection, or a collection which changes frequently (as for example a current affairs file), or a collection of computer files or websites which are not kept on a shelf where they can easily be browsed. In all of these cases, when confronted with a situation which requires you to find information quickly, you may feel rather like the Bagthorpes when confronted with all those anonymous tin cans. The information you want must be available somewhere – but how do you locate it?

In most cases, the quickest way to find out is to consult the catalogue. If it is inaccurate, lacking in essential details or simply non-existent, you may still be able to find the information, object or document for which you are searching, but the search will use up a great deal of valuable time which could have been better spent doing other things.

A library without a catalogue is rather like a town without a sewer; you may get away with it for a while, but sooner or later something will start to smell. The bigger the town, the bigger the smell.

Foskett (1982) puts it rather more elegantly:

... instead of the individual store of knowledge, we have the corporate store: the library; instead of the individual memory, we have the corporate memory: library catalogues and bibliographical tools. And just as the individual whose memory fails him cannot pass on wanted information when it is wanted, *so a library whose corporate memory is inadequate will fail in its purpose.* (emphasis mine)

What the catalogue is for

Cataloguing is the art (or, some might say, the science) of describing a document or object in the smallest possible number of words. Catalogues, like libraries and information services, vary in their size and complexity, from the handlist of books in a school library to OCLC's Worldcat database, an online union catalogue of over 30 million records from libraries around the world.

Catalogues have been around for some time. The earliest known cataloguer is Callimachus, who compiled a bibliography of Greek literature held in the great library at Alexandria around 240 BC. However, the standardisation of cataloguing took rather longer (and is still incomplete). The first published guidelines for cataloguing were Panizzi's rules for compiling the British Museum catalogue, included as an introduction to the printed catalogue in 1841.

The next giant leap forward was the publication of Cutter's *Rules for a Printed Dictionary Catalog* (1876). Although this predates the advent of computer catalogues, Cutter's general comments on the principles of cataloguing are still relevant today:

> ... the preparation of a catalogue must vary as it is to be manuscript or printed, and, if the latter, as it is to be merely an index to the library, giving in the shortest possible compass clues by which the public can find books, or is to attempt to furnish more information on various points, or finally is to be made with a certain regard to what may be called style.

This idea was further developed in 1908 with the publication of the first Anglo-American cataloguing code; its influence is still to be seen in the Anglo-American Cataloguing Rules' (AACR) three levels of descriptive cataloguing. The use of computers in cataloguing and the advent of shared databases like the Online Computer Library Center (OCLC) provided added impetus to the process of standardisation. Today, there are many different resources for cataloguers to use in their work: name authority lists, subject thesauri and various internationally accepted cataloguing standards, the most important of which for our purposes are the International Standard for Bibliographic Description (ISBD), AACR and the Dublin Core.

As the basic purpose of any catalogue is, firstly, to provide a record of what resources are available in the collection or collections being described and, secondly, to enable users of the collection to find information on the subjects they are interested in, the task of cataloguing may be broken down into two parts:

1. descriptive cataloguing;

2. subject cataloguing.

Descriptive Cataloging: "Item I: One
Booke. Item II: Also an Booke, larger..."

Descriptive cataloguing may be further broken down into two stages:

(a) constructing a bibliographic description of the item in hand which is sufficiently detailed to distinguish it from all other items with similar characteristics (e.g. the same author or title);

(b) making entries for the author/s, title/s and series in the appropriate indexes.

Subject Cataloging: "File this one under
'gore', 'blood' and 'sheer bad taste'..."

Subject cataloguing, unlike indexing, is intended to provide an overview of the most important subjects which a document deals with, not a detailed analysis. It is usually not necessary to read (watch, listen to) the whole thing in order to do this; a glance at the title page, the list of contents and the synopsis (or equivalents) is usually sufficient, although sometimes the introduction and/or the conclusion must be checked as well.

The whole process is intended to answer two questions: firstly, what is this item? secondly, what is it about?

The three virtues of a good catalogue are:

■ accuracy;

■ clarity;

■ consistency.

Accuracy is even more important in a computer catalogue than in a card catalogue – a mistyped catalogue card may still be usable (and, given that it will be filed by a human being, may even be in the right place in the file) but a mistyped or wrongly coded computer record could be lost forever. Clarity is equally important; it should be obvious to anyone who looks at the catalogue record which fields refer to the title, author, publication details, etc., and the subject of the work described should be clear from the subject descriptors. Finally, consistency is what separates a good catalogue from a mediocre or bad one. An author's works should be consolidated under one name heading which is unique to that person (or organisation) – your users do not want to wade through all the possible spellings of

Shakespeare to find out whether you have a copy of *Romeo and Juliet*, or scroll through 216 entries under T. Jones to find the works of the particular T. Jones they are interested in. Also, materials on the same subject should be described using the same subject keywords or headings.

Catalogues have come a long way since Callimachus. 'Dictionary' catalogues (printed lists of materials in a particular library or collection) are still produced. Card indexes are still used in some smaller libraries, as they are easier to create and maintain than computer catalogues. Computer catalogues are the norm in large and medium-sized libraries; many smaller libraries have also chosen this option. Yet the basic purpose of the catalogue remains the same, whether the catalogue describes a collection of documents and/or objects held in one particular location or a collection of materials available on a particular subject from a number of different sources, or is an attempt to provide a description of every document in the world (OCLC is the nearest we are ever going to get to that...). Catalogues are there to help people find the information they want quickly and efficiently. All the complicated rules, all the agonising over standards and the quibbles over the correct subject terms to use are means to this end. It is easy to forget and get bogged down in the details or distracted by the beautiful shining edifice of metadata which you are creating but it is important to remember, as you labour over a particularly arcane and apparently unrewarding piece of cataloguing, that your work is helping your colleagues at the information desk and/or your users to find the documents they need.

Anticipating the needs of users

Anticipating the needs of the user:
"Absolutely anything on curses, as quick as you can!"

Somewhere in cataloguer's heaven there exists an Ideal Catalogue which perfectly describes every item in the celestial library in the greatest detail allowed by the cataloguing rules. Down here in the 'real' world, every time you create a catalogue record you have to make a trade-off between the time you actually have available to do the work and the amount of detail you need to put in so that users of the catalogue can find the item on the library shelves. In theory, the trade-off should be the same for everything; in practice, you will probably find that it pays to be aware of your users' needs. Otherwise you may find yourself wasting time putting in unnecessary details, or alternatively leaving out vital information and wasting other people's time in unneccessarily complicated searches. The catalogue record for a video destined for a public library's AV collection may differ considerably from the record for a copy of the same video held at an academic library with a large research collection for film and drama, for example.

The stereotype of a cataloguer is of someone hunched over a computer (or possibly a typewriter) in a back room, entirely surrounded by books. Your work space may very well look like this, but it is important to be aware of the needs of the people who benefit from your labours. Knowing what kind of information your end users are interested in will help you become a better cataloguer, if only because you will get a better sense of what to leave out. If you are the only information professional in your organisation, you will not have to worry about being isolated from your users; your job will naturally involve answering queries and helping people to find the materials they need. If you work in a larger information service where cataloguing and reference work are done by different people, it is worth asking about the possibility of doing some work on the enquiry desk; if this is not feasible, ask your colleagues to keep you informed of suggestions on how the catalogue could be improved.

In addition to being aware of the needs of your users, it is important to promote the catalogue to them. This is easier to do in an academic or special library than in a public library, where a complicated search is more likely to be done by a librarian acting as an intermediary for the end user, but if the people who use the library are unaware of the potential of the catalogue they will not use it to its full capability. To give an example from my own experience: from 1996 to 2003 I have been working on the retrospective cataloguing of Reading University Library's rare book collections. The University has an active and highly respected Department of Typography and Graphic Communication and is also the home of the Centre for Writing, Printing and Publishing History, so there is a large concentration of researchers interested in the history of books and printing. The records I was creating for early printed books therefore included a lot of information on publishers, printers and illustrators, descriptions of bindings and evidence of previous owners, in addition to the usual bibliographic and subject information. In 2001/2002, concerned that potential users of the collections were unaware of the amount of information held in the catalogue records for these items, I gave several talks for staff and students in which I explained what information was accessible and how to search for it in the catalogue. At the time of writing, it is too early to say whether this has had a measurable effect on use of the rare books, but what is certain is that use of the fully catalogued parts of the collections has increased.

To sum up: it is not enough to be aware of the needs of your users and to adjust your cataloguing procedures so that the information in the catalogue is tailored to their requirements. You must also ensure that they know enough about the catalogue to be able to use it effectively. In an academic or special library, this will probably involve training the end users to search the catalogue themselves; in a public library it is more likely to be the library staff who need to be kept aware of cataloguing developments.

Convincing your boss that cataloguing is important

There is no longer any guarantee that a manager who is also a librarian will be sympathetic to your difficulties and/or understand what you actually do. Many library administrators (even those who are qualified librarians) think that automation of cataloguing has made it easy enough for a trained monkey to do. In reality, it is becoming more difficult for libraries with unusual and/or research collections to find suitable staff to catalogue their material, as the pool of professional cataloguers is shrinking; several libraries involved in the Research Support Libraries Programme (RSLP) experienced difficulties in recruitment for their retrospective cataloguing projects. Yet the dazzling displays of rapid information retrieval of which our colleagues in Information Services are justly proud would be impossible without the painstaking work of cataloguers.

Convincing the boss:
"Oh yeah, before we got the system you could never find a thumbscrew when you needed one."

Bowman (2003) identifies the two most common cataloguing fallacies thus:

> Ever since computers began to be used in cataloguing ... there has been a school of thought that in some mysterious way computers would be able to do all the cataloguing that was necessary, and that it would no longer be necessary to employ human cataloguers ... Another fallacy about cataloguing is this: that it is simply a matter of following rules without using any

thought. This implies that very little training is required for cataloguers, and that cataloguers can therefore be employed on very low salary grades.

These two assumptions are closely related, because one thing which computers are very good at is following rules. If you program a computer to do X in a particular situation, it will do X for as long as it is in working order or until you tell it to do Y. It will not get bored and start making careless mistakes, or demand a pay rise, or go off and get a more interesting job, as a human might do. The difficulty with getting a computer to do cataloguing is that it is not always clear in a given situation whether you should apply rule X or rule Y. Human cataloguers will use their discretion, based on their knowledge of how the world works, their experience of having catalogued similar items in the past, their best guess at what the writers of the rules they are using intended to happen, and their estimate of what solution will be most helpful to the users of the library. One day, perhaps, someone will create a computer program which can do all of this and costs less to employ than a human, but we aren't quite there yet.

Administrators and managers are naturally concerned with keeping costs down, and cataloguing is a prime target for the cost-conscious manager. It is the most expensive process a document will go through when being added to the library stock. Just to give you some idea of how much it costs, a longitudinal study carried out by Iowa State University Library found that the average cost per title catalogued between 1987 and 1990 was $16.53, including items which had been recatalogued (Morris, 1992). When these were excluded, the cost per (newly acquired) title rose to $20.01; in some cases this would be more than the cost of buying the document. Cutting the amount of staff time devoted to cataloguing or downgrading cataloguing posts so that cataloguing is wholly or partly carried out by clerical staff rather than trained professionals seems an obvious way to save money, and you may find yourself in the position of having to defend your work every time the budget is considered. This is not necessarily a bad thing; in some circumstances it may be useful to examine what you are doing and ask yourself 'Can we/I do better? Is there a way of streamlining the cataloguing process to make it more efficient?' On the other hand, if you have to do it every year, it becomes wearing.

You may find the following list of points useful:

1. Cataloguing adds value to a collection. If you don't know what you've got, how can you exploit your resources properly? If you spend £20.00 on a document and no one knows it's in the library because it isn't on the catalogue, then the money has been wasted. Library resources are there to be used; if no one knows about them, they won't be!

2. Some cataloguing is easy. Some is very difficult indeed. The quality of the catalogue is going to depend on the skill and knowledge of the person or persons doing the cataloguing.

3. Cataloguers prefer to follow internationally agreed standards for cataloguing because this makes it easy to exchange records between different catalogues. If someone else has a copy of the new document in your library already

catalogued, you can duplicate their record instead of having to do it all over again from scratch. This saves money. Using an internationally recognised standard also makes it easier for other people to understand your catalogue.

4. Cataloguing is expensive because it is labour-intensive, and also because the people required to do it are highly trained and (hopefully) highly paid. It is possible to save money by employing unqualified staff to download and/or input records, but unless their work is supervised by a professional or experienced paraprofessional the quality of the catalogue will suffer.

5. Switching from card cataloguing to computer cataloguing does save some time (and therefore money), but the most time-consuming and expensive part of cataloguing any item is deciding what should go into the record and checking the headings you are going to use, and this takes about the same amount of time when working on a computer as typing catalogue cards used to. There are some savings to be made: catalogue records can be imported from other systems rather than created from scratch, and there is no longer any need to spend hours filing catalogue cards. The advent of online authority files has made it possible to check and validate headings without moving from your desk, but no one has yet invented a computer program which can speed up the process of deciding what headings to put in the record in the first place.

6. The real incentive for using a computer rather than a card catalogue comes after the catalogue record has been created. Because computers allow keyword as well as

index searching, the online computer catalogue offers a much wider choice of access points than a card index and therefore gives a better service to the user. Also, because the computer catalogue may be made available over the Internet, it is not necessary to visit the library in order to use the catalogue.

You could also suggest that your boss shadows you for a day or half a day to find out what you actually do – make sure you have a good representative selection of materials to work on. If all else fails, pray for a computer crash. If the catalogue is unavailable for a few days it may help the sceptics in your organisation to realise how much they rely on it.

2

What to catalogue?

Stop ill-using your professionally educated brain to make individual bibliographic records and start making catalogs... There are too few of us thinking about what catalogs should look like and how they should work.

Hoerman (2002)

I don't know much about cataloguing, but I know what I like...

Now that we have established the importance of the catalogue as a tool for finding information held by your organisation, we move on to consider precisely what information the catalogue should contain. The amount of information in each catalogue record will vary depending on the type of library your catalogue is designed to serve and/or the importance of the document (or object) to your users. The amount of information in individual fields of the catalogue record will also vary depending on the type of document being catalogued; for example, when cataloguing a map you would normally include its scale in the catalogue record, but this information is either unnecessary or completely irrelevant for other formats.

It is normally considered good practice to move from the general to the particular, but in this chapter, what I have to say about cataloguing policy and how to decide what should be recorded in catalogue records will make more sense if I first discuss the different types of information which may be recorded in an individual record.

What a catalogue record contains

Records in a library catalogue contain information in three categories:

- *bibliographic description* – identifying features of the document;
- *access points* – keywords or headings describing the subject of the document: names of persons responsible for the document, e.g. the author/s, editor/s, illustrator/s, publisher/printer, etc.;
- *'enhancements'* – additional information on the document, e.g. abstract, list of contents, image or sound file, link to URL, etc.

A suggested list of common elements in each category follows, together with examples of how each level of description would be applied to an imaginary document. I have used a book as my example; Chapter 5 will deal with the subject of how to describe documents in different formats.

Bibliographic description

Bibliographic description

A basic record will usually contain the following information:

- title
- author/s and other persons responsible for the content of the book
- edition
- publication details
- series
- format
- identification number.

The relative importance of each piece of information will vary depending on the format of the document. For example, it is not usually necessary to include information about which edition of an online resource you are cataloguing because the version available online is normally both the most current and the only one available. Similarly, it is not always possible to identify the author of a document, either because it was published anonymously or because it was the work of many different authors, none of whom could be said to have a definitive 'voice' in the final production. On the other hand, it is usually important to have a title of some description; in cases where there is none (for example, when cataloguing objects) you will probably wish to supply one yourself in the interests of clarity. Format is not particularly important in the description of texts,[1] but in the case of audio-visual and electronic resources it is vital in helping the catalogue user to find relevant and useable information.

So, a basic description of *Dentures of Desire* by Cynthia Lustgirdle might look like this:

Title	Dentures of desire
Author, etc.	Cynthia Lustgirdle
Publication	London: Cursed Powderpuff Press, 2003
Series	Pinnacles of passion
Format	Text
ISBN	132456257123X[2]

The edition statement is omitted in this instance because there is none (it is the first Cursed Powderpuff edition).

A more detailed record might also include information on:

- physical size and extent of object – number of pages, running time (for audio and video recordings), etc.;
- illustrations (for printed documents);
- distribution details;
- language.

The size or length of a document is more important for audio and video recordings than it is for print materials, although there are situations when it can be useful to know how big a given item is, as anyone who has searched for a lost book could tell you. Distribution details may be included for non-book materials like DVDs and videos, but are usually unnecessary for books.

The language of a document is a useful piece of information to have in a catalogue for a multilingual collection; there is no point in retrieving 200 records for documents on snail farming in outer Mongolia if 180 of them are in Mandarin Chinese and you (or your client) can only read English.

Returning to our example, an expanded version of the catalogue record might look like this (new fields and parts of fields are in italics):

Title	Dentures of desire
Author, etc.	Cynthia Lustgirdle; *illustrated by William Rembrandt Robinson*
Publication	London: Cursed Powderpuff Press, 2003
Series	Pinnacles of passion
Format	Text
ISBN	132456257123X
Size/extent	*452 p., 23 cm*
Illustrations	*1 coloured plate (frontispiece)*
Language	*English*

Distribution details are omitted as being unimportant for books. Note that the 'Author, etc.' field has been expanded with the name of the illustrator as well as that of the author, in the form in which they appear on the title page: ISBD calls this part of the bibliographic description the *statement of responsibility* rather than the author statement, precisely because the persons, corporate bodies or multi-tentacled alien entities named on the title page (or equivalent) as being responsible for the content of the document are not all necessarily authors: they may also be editors, illustrators or compilers.

The cataloguing equivalent of a Rolls-Royce would include all the above information (where relevant) together with:

- printing details;
- history of this and any previous editions;
- references to published descriptions of this title;
- descriptions of annotations, inscriptions, insertions...;
- description of binding.

It is unlikely that you will find it necessary to catalogue items to this level of detail unless you are working on rare books or archival collections. However, if you wanted to do this for Cynthia's book, you would end up with something resembling the following record:

Title	Dentures of desire
Author, etc.	Cynthia Lustgirdle; illustrated by William Rembrandt Robinson
Publication	London: Cursed Powderpuff Press, 2003
Series	Pinnacles of passion
Format	Text
ISBN	132456257123X
Size/extent	452 p., 23 cm
Illustrations	1 coloured plate (frontispiece)

Language	English
Printer	*Printed by Joseph Bloggs*
Editions	*First published in 1926 by the Gargoyle Press; this edition is limited to 250 copies*
Inscriptions etc.	*Signed by the author; presented to the library by Gillian Smith in memory of her mother Elizabeth Smith (aka Cynthia Lustgirdle)*
Binding	*Publisher's original paper binding*

... and so on ad infinitum.

Cynthia Lustgirdle signs copies of her new bestseller 'Dentures of Desire'

Access points

This is the technical term for the words in the catalogue record which enable users of the catalogue to find the items they are interested in. In the days of dictionary and card catalogues, they were provided via an alphabetical index or series of indexes and providing extra access points for items in the catalogue was a rather laborious process. In the case of a dictionary catalogue, each additional access point took up at least one extra line; in the case of a card catalogue, it meant writing or typing extra cards. The additional entries usually had brief details of the document and a reference to the 'main entry', which was the entry under the name of the main author or the title (for a document without an author). The catalogue user would then have to find the main entry for that document to see the full details.

Computer catalogues are able to provide keyword searching as well as index searching and so every word in the catalogue record is potentially an 'access point'. Most library systems also have the capacity to provide browseable alphabetical indexes. The majority of catalogue users will normally prefer to use a simple keyword search to locate records, but an alphabetical index is helpful for some types of search (e.g. finding all the holdings by a particular author). It is usually worth having even if the only people who use it are the library staff themselves, as the cost of the labour involved in creating extra name and subject headings (once the indexing has been set up) is negligible compared to the benefits of improved access to the record; they all refer back to the same bibliographic information, which only has to be typed once. In addition to this, if you have a catalogue with a web user interface it should be possible to provide hyperlink searching for name and subject headings (and even series titles); this allows users to click on the headings when they have found a document which interests them to find whether there are other documents on the same subject, by the same author or in the same series in the catalogue.

It is assumed that the library system would be programmed to provide keyword access to the following fields in the record, if present:

- author
- title
- subject
- series
- editor/s
- illustrator/s.

A more detailed catalogue would also provide keyword access to any notes or abstracts.

The access points referred to in the following list are those which could be included in an alphabetical index.

A *very* basic record would contain the following access points:

- author or authors (if any);
- title.

The simplest catalogue might omit all but the first named author on the title page, and only index titles for items which have no author.

Continuing with the same example, the access points for *Dentures of Desire* in a simple catalogue would be:

Author	Lustgirdle, Cynthia
Title	Dentures of desire

A more detailed catalogue would include access points for:

- editor/s;
- series title;
- subject and/or genre.

Many libraries prefer to provide subject access via the shelf location rather than subject keywords or headings in the catalogue record. This is a good approach provided that your library stocks only documents which are on one clearly definable subject and which will not be of interest to anyone wanting information on other subjects. Unfortunately, most modern libraries do not fall into this category, as Coates (1988) remarks:

> The expression 'distinct subject' had more meaning to Cutter and his contemporaries than it can have to us. At that time knowledge still consisted of a number of accepted spheres of thought, each comfortably separate from the others. 'Subjects' were islands of knowledge separated from one another by oceanic voids ... In our day the various islands have become so thoroughly interconnected that it is often very difficult to see any ocean at all.

Subject access is particularly useful for documents on multi-disciplinary subjects such as globalisation, or for documents which could be said to cover two or more subjects in equal depth.

Cynthia's book is actually a work of fiction, but there is no reason why fiction should not be given subject or genre keywords if desired, provided that there is a clear distinction made in the catalogue between fiction and non-fiction titles relating to the same subjects.

The access points for Cynthia's book would now look something like this:

Author	Lustgirdle, Cynthia
Title	Dentures of desire
Series	*Pinnacles of passion*
Subject	*Dentists (Fiction)*
Genre	*Romantic fiction*

The access points for an equally imaginary non-fiction book on dentists might look like this:

Title	Twenty years behind the drill: dentists' reminiscences
Editor	*Cranworthy, G.A.*
Subject	*Dentists (Biography)*

A very detailed catalogue record might add entries for the:

- illustrator
- printer
- publisher
- any identifiable previous owners
- binder
- translator
- book designer.

This level of detail is useful for early printed books and manuscripts and may be included in records for other documents which form part of 'special' or archival collections but is not often necessary for standard materials.

Author	Lustgirdle, Cynthia
Title	Dentures of desire
Series	Pinnacles of passion
Subject	Dentists (Fiction)
Genre	Romantic fiction
Illustrator	*Robinson, William Rembrandt*
Publisher	*Cursed Powderpuff Press*
Previous owner	*Smith, Gillian*

For non-print materials such as sound and video recordings, it might be appropriate to add the names of the principal performers (the soloists in a music recording or the stars of a film, for example). In addition to these, it might be considered useful to have access points for physical characteristics of the document, for example to allow catalogue users to identify documents by type of binding. This question will be discussed more fully in Chapter 8.

Enhancements

These are things which you would not normally expect to find attached to a catalogue record. They would not be provided in a basic catalogue, but now that it is possible to provide web interfaces for library catalogues it is also possible to add extra information which may be either accessed via a hyperlink in the catalogue record or included in the record itself. They include:

- abstracts;

- images;

- sound files;

- tables of contents;

- hyperlink to full text of document.

The benefits of having these enhancements are obvious; abstracts and tables of contents provide extra subject access to the documents they describe, sound files might be provided to allow users to sample music CDs before deciding whether to borrow them; images could be included for the bindings of early printed books and would be particularly valuable for anyone searching a catalogue of a collection of objects; it is far easier to show a picture of a Babylonian demon bowl than to explain in words exactly what it is and how this particular demon bowl differs from the 500 others in the collection you are cataloguing. Links to the full text of the document are of course only possible if you have it available in electronic form!

There are two things to watch out for if you are considering adding enhancements such as these to your catalogue. The first is copyright. You need to check with your organisation's copyright expert (and, if s/he doesn't know, with someone who does) whether what you want to do will violate the copyright laws. Providing sound files of parts of CDs almost certainly will! Scanning a book you have into a PDF file so that you can provide the full text online is also illegal unless you have obtained the agreement of the copyright holder to do this, just as photocopying all of it would be. The second thing to ask before you start is whether the enhancement to the catalogue is really going to be worth the extra work you will have to put in. Is there another way of getting at the same information which will cost less? For example, is there an online database you can subscribe to which would allow you to search tables of contents from the journals you subscribe to without having to scan them into your catalogue records?

In the case of Cynthia's book, you might wish to provide an image of the cover linked to the catalogue record, or scan in the publisher's blurb on the back cover for the edification of your catalogue users. Providing pictures of your documents does at least avoid the following situation...

"I'm looking for a
big, red book..."

Carved in stone? Writing a catalogue policy for your organisation

This brings us neatly onto the subject of cataloguing policy. As Hoerman remarks, cataloguing policy is something which is easily neglected in the rush to get materials catalogued and available to library users as quickly as possible. When you don't have time to keep up with your routine work, how can you possibly find time to sit down and think about what you are doing and why you are doing it?

The answer is that you can't really afford not to. It is pointless to waste time and energy in trying to keep up with cataloguing throughput if the records you are creating are deficient in some way – containing unnecessary detail, for example. Sitting down and taking a long hard look at what you are doing and asking yourself whether it is really necessary or desirable to do it that way and if there is a better way of doing the work could save you more time than you lose in thinking.

A formal cataloguing policy serves two purposes:

- If the cataloguing department consists of more than one person, it formalises their working practice and ensures that everyone understands the Right Way To Do Things.
- It is available for reference when other members of the organisation ask what the cataloguers do all day and/or why the catalogue works the way it does.

A cataloguing policy, even a written one, should not be treated as if it has been carved in stone. It should be periodically reviewed and changed as necessary.

You will need to begin by asking again the key questions from Chapter 1:

1. Who are the users of the library?
2. What are their information needs?
3. How can the catalogue help them?

You should then make a list of every piece of information which you consider might be useful in identifying and locating documents in your library, referring to the checklist given above. That is your ideal catalogue record.

Since we do not live in an ideal world, you will then need to consider the following questions:

1. How many new documents are acquired in an average year?

2. How much cataloguing time is available to process them?[3]

If the number of documents acquired is greater than the maximum number which can be catalogued to the standard you want in the time available, you will have to compromise. Look again at your Ideal Catalogue Record and ask yourself these questions:

1. Is all this information absolutely necessary? Is there anything we could do without?

2. Are there any categories of documents which could be catalogued to a less exacting standard?

When you have finished, you will (hopefully) have a realistic cataloguing policy with achievable aims.

In order to see how this might work in practice, let's consider the case of the (imaginary) public library of Much Gossip in Nowhereshire with 10,000 new acquisitions a year and one full-time cataloguer. In an ideal world, the policy-makers decide that the catalogue record for each new item should include the following:

- author/s
- title
- editor/s
- publication details
- edition
- physical size
- format
- language
- series
- subject.

Assuming that the cataloguer works 1,610 hours (230 days) in the year, this would mean that he or she would have to average slightly more than six items an hour or approximately 44 per day in order to keep up with new acquisitions. This is achievable if all the materials being catalogued are straightforward and it is possible to download and edit records for them from elsewhere, but it is an unrealistic target for complicated materials and/or original cataloguing. The policy-makers reluctantly abandon their 'ideal world' and look again at the information they want in each catalogue record. They decide to leave out the following:

- language – the vast majority of materials in the library are in English;
- physical size – this is useful in some circumstances, but not essential;

- format – *except* for audio-visual materials, where it is essential both to identify the document and to enable users of the library to identify the materials they want.

They also decide to have special rules for the following categories:

- *children's books* – will not have subject entries because most children using the library browse the shelves to locate non-fiction rather than checking the catalogue;

- *CD-Roms and other electronic media* – system requirements and conditions of use will be added to the catalogue record;

- *local history collection* – records will include information on former owners of the documents and detailed subject access to their content.

This still leaves the cataloguer with a big job – the work on the local history collection will expand to fill the time available to do it – but provided that the majority of documents being catalogued are straightforward it is doable. It does, however, leave no time for anything but new cataloguing – no time for attending meetings, training others in the use of the catalogue, upgrading old records or catalogue maintenance.

If the department consists of more
than 1 person... "It must have been
a terrible strain on her. In the end
she just filed everything under
'Cheese' and fled the country"

Into the abyss: the politics of cataloguing

You might think that this would be all about office politics, but in fact the 'politics' of cataloguing is really about how you describe the objects and documents you are working on. Ideally you should refrain from making editorial comment and describe what you see as objectively as possible. This might involve not correcting typographical errors on the title page, or finding neutral words to describe the subject of a document whose conclusions you violently disagree with.

The ideal of subject cataloguing is to describe the subject in terms which are used by people who are interested in that subject so that they will know what you are talking about. Assuming you are using a controlled vocabulary (where there is only one approved term for describing a subject and all other possible equivalents are given as cross-references) this will mean updating your subject headings when the approved term changes. For example, at the beginning of the nineteenth century the subject now known as economics was called political economy. No one would now expect to find materials on economics described in the library catalogue as 'Political economy'. In the late twentieth century, a number of subjects which had either not existed before or had never been considered important enough to require detailed analysis suddenly leapt into prominence and library catalogues (and classification schemes, but that is another story) had to be changed to reflect this. Examples include computer science, globalisation and ecology.

Politics of Cataloguing:
"We want to know why you put
'Rites of the Illuminati' in the
fiction section..."

If you are not using a controlled vocabulary for subject keywords, maintaining subject headings is not a problem because when the 'approved' subject terms change you simply switch to the new words without changing anything in the old records. However, although this will save you time it will create a problem for the users of the catalogue, because when they search for subject keywords the system will only retrieve records with the term (old or new) which they typed in, so they will not find all the materials available on that particular subject unless they know all the terms which might be used to describe the subject, and are also aware that they need to do a separate search for each one. If you have a sophisticated computer system, it might be possible to program it either to automatically search for alternative terms as well as the one input by the catalogue user, or to offer a list of alternative terms when it presents the results of the search. Of course, this in itself will be time-consuming, because you will need to reprogram the computer every time a subject keyword changes in order to add more alternatives to the list, and if your computer system is a basic one, you will not be able to use this solution anyway and will have to resort to leaving notices beside the computer terminals and giving out lists of subject synonyms.

Most large libraries which use controlled subject vocabularies use Library of Congress Subject Headings (LCSH). This creates a further problem, because LCSH is an American system and therefore (naturally) uses American terms to describe subjects which may not be the same as the words you and your users would normally employ. The difference is most noticeable in education; LCSH describes primary schools as elementary schools, head teachers are principals, and so on. The conscientious cataloguer is then faced with a dilemma: should he or she stick to the controlled vocabulary, even though it will create problems for the catalogue users, or abandon the 'approved' term for local use and create headings which will be understandable to the users? In recent years, LCSH has been revised in an attempt to make the terms less culture-specific, but in the case of education any attempt to revise the terms to make them understandable to Europeans would make them incomprehensible to Americans. There is no easy answer to this question: you will have to choose the best solution for your local situation.

Objectivity in choosing subject terms is sometimes difficult to maintain. Take the book illustrated in Figure 2.1 as an example. This is an Italian translation of an English text, *Protocols of the Wise Men of Zion*, which appeared in 1920. It is basically an anti-Semitic tract claiming to give evidence of a global Jewish conspiracy, a very famous anti-Semitic tract in fact. The question facing the cataloguer is this: should the book be catalogued on its own terms, using only the evidence for what it is about which is presented in the text, or should the cataloguer add something in the record – a note or an extra subject term – to show that the work is considered (at least) controversial? In the past, cataloguers were more ready to add editorial comments such as 'Controversial literature' to records: nowadays we are more hesitant (or less arrogant) and usually restrain ourselves. In this particular instance, one could make a case for adding something to the catalogue record to warn the unwary reader what he or she is in for, but many cataloguers would argue that even for this item, expressing opinions about the content of the work in the catalogue is unjustifiable.

Figure 2.1 Title page of *L'Internazionale ebraica* (*Protocols of the Wise Men of Zion*)

Notes

1. See Chapter 8 for an exception to this rule.

2. ISBNs are normally 10 digits long, but 13-digit numbers have been approved and are beginning to be used.

3. See Chapter 3 for guidance on how to estimate cataloguing time required.

Who should catalogue?

...no professional cataloguer should be spending most of his or her time making out dreadfully short standard bibliographic records.

Hoerman (2002)

The perfect cataloguer is an expert on all subjects, fluent in all world languages and familiar with every writing system ever used. He or she is also an expert on computers, has memorised all the cataloguing manuals and coding necessary to do the job and can type 200 words per minute with no typographical errors.

The perfect cataloguer:
"Well he's all right, but he's hardly ideal..."

Well, cataloguing has to be done by real human beings. It also has to be paid for by cost-conscious library administrators, so you will need to look carefully at ways of cutting cataloguing costs without compromising on the quality of your records.

The process of cataloguing

> ...intricate ritual faultlessly performed...
>
> Dorothy Sayers, *The Nine Tailors*

Cataloguing and records management may be roughly broken down into three main processes:

- bibliographic description;
- subject cataloguing;
- authority control.

Bibliographic description

This is (usually!) the most straightforward part of the process and may be delegated to a library assistant or paraprofessional. This does not mean that bibliographic description is always easy or that the person doing it will not require supervision and assistance from someone more highly qualified. It may even be more appropriate for an information professional to do bibliographic description of some materials. For example, many libraries prefer to have their audiovisual materials dealt with entirely by professionals and cataloguers of early printed books or manuscripts will deal with bibliographic description themselves rather than delegating the job to assistants. The key question to ask when deciding whether materials in a particular category are suitable for a library assistant to catalogue is: 'How easy is it to tell which bits of information in the document refer to the author, title, publisher...?' The title page of a book presents information in a highly structured format which is (usually!) easy to understand. It is not always quite so easy to understand how to transfer the information about a video or an object into a catalogue record.

This part of the job calls for someone with good communication skills and a passion for those niggling little details of punctuation and spelling which so often catch out even the most intelligent people. However, the process of bibliographic description also requires someone who is able to transcribe what is actually there in the document rather than what he or she thinks should be there – sometimes a word in the title may be deliberately misspelled, for example. The bibliographic description should preserve the spelling as seen in the document rather than the word as normally spelled by the cataloguer. This requires the type of person who makes a good witness in a murder case – someone who is clear about what he or she has seen and is not inclined to make up a better version to please his or her audience.

Other useful attributes for bibliographic description are a broad general knowledge (it helps when determining the country of publication to know that Monaco is an independent principality, for example) and a good memory for the cataloguing rules (if you have to look everything up all the time, it slows you down).

Subject cataloguing

This is the intellectual process of assigning subject headings or keywords to each document. It should be done by an information professional, ideally one who has some knowledge of the subject being catalogued. In an organisation where bibliographic description has been delegated to a library assistant, the information professional responsible for creating subject entries should also be checking the rest of the computer record, adding extra name headings and correcting the library assistant's work where necessary.

The most important attribute for a subject cataloguer is good analytical skills. It is helpful to have an in-depth knowledge of the subject or subjects you will be cataloguing, but it is more important to be able to describe the subject of a given document concisely and accurately. Knowing the subject will only help you describe the document accurately, and may even be a barrier in the way of a concise description.

The second requirement is that you should have a working knowledge of the languages in which the documents you are cataloguing have been written (or filmed, or recorded). It is not absolutely essential to know a language in order to catalogue documents in it (I have catalogued books in Hebrew, Armenian and Polish, without ever having learned any of these languages) but if you are often called on to catalogue materials in another language it pays to learn enough so that you can get the gist of the subject.

"I told you the occult books should have a section of their own."

Authority control

This involves ensuring that name and subject headings are used consistently in the catalogue and that all authorised headings conform to whatever standards the library has adopted. It is usually the responsibility of the most senior cataloguer of the organisation, although other cataloguers may work on authority records. It makes the difference between a mediocre catalogue and a good one.

The most important requirement for someone responsible for authority control is a commitment to maintaining standards. Authority control is the cataloguer's quality assurance; in fact, Hoerman has suggested that we should abandon the term altogether and rename it 'Heading Access Assurance' (Hoerman, 2002). I actually prefer the term 'quality control', as this has the merit of being understandable by non-librarians.

The person responsible for quality control in a catalogue will also need endless patience (even more than the average cataloguer) and a penchant for opening cans of worms that others would prefer to ignore...

It is useful to know as much as possible about how the computer system works. Authority control usually involves working at a higher level within the system than when inputting ordinary bibliographic records, and the more you know about systems and computer programs the better.

We thus have a 'cataloguing team' of three hypothetical people: Doris Dogsbody the library assistant, Patrick Putupon the professional cataloguer and Hermione Hawkeye the head cataloguer. Of course, most organisations have either many more cataloguers than this or only one person who is expected to do everything, but each part of the cataloguing process calls for slightly different skills, as we have seen.

How long does it take to catalogue a document?

Never mind all this bureaucracy, you say, how long does it take to catalogue a single book? This is rather like asking 'how long is a piece of string?' The answer is dependent on a number of factors, including;

- how good you are – the skill and experience of the cataloguer;

- whether it's been done before – does the catalogue record have to be created entirely from scratch, or can it be copied from somewhere else?

- how good the record needs to be – the level of detail required to describe that particular item.

Before you throw up your hands in horror and wish you had chosen an easier job like lion-taming or teaching instead, let me reassure you that your cataloguing speed will increase as you learn more about the job and the subjects of the materials you are working with. Another strategy for improving your speed is to copy a record for the item in hand from somewhere else, either by downloading it onto your system from another library which has already catalogued the same document, or alternatively by copying a record for a similar document from your own database – the previous edition of the same book, for example, or another book by the same author – and editing the new record as necessary. Most systems will also allow you to set up templates for original cataloguing, which saves a little typing time and wear and tear on your fingers.

The really big variable in this equation is the level of detail required for the item in hand. A work of fiction by a well-known author whose other works are already on your database could take as little as five minutes to catalogue from start to finish. At the other extreme, a fifteenth-century printed book with hand-illuminated capitals and a large number of bookplates and autographs of previous owners to record could take anything up to half a day to catalogue thoroughly. Somewhere in between those two extremes are the academic texts with complicated subjects, the multimedia kits with a hundred different parts, the websites, the skeletons, the pictures and sound recordings. Also the serials, which are a whole different ball game.

Here are some estimates of cataloguing times:

- *1–2 books per hour.* This may sound like a snail's pace, but it is my usual speed when cataloguing early printed books and other items from Reading University Library's Special Collections. The extra time is needed for two reasons: firstly, it is all original cataloguing as we do not download records for Special Collections items; secondly, a considerable amount of detail is added to Special Collections records which is not necessary for other catalogue records. Two books an hour would be a reasonable speed to expect a novice cataloguer or a cataloguer who is doing mainly original cataloguing to achieve.

- *3–4 books per hour.* This is the average speed of cataloguers at Reading University Library, although some of the most experienced can achieve five books per hour. Records are downloaded from a bibliographic records supplier for most items (though many foreign-language texts have to have catalogue records created from scratch) and this target speed allows plenty of time for checking and upgrading records.

- *5–8 books per hour.* Achievable if you are using high-quality downloaded records for most materials and/or the cataloguer is very experienced. My personal sporting best for original cataloguing is seven books per hour, but the items I was working on when I achieved this speed were very straightforward! This allows some time for editing records, but if they are to be of a high standard (for a research library, for example) it would be better to set a slightly lower target.

- *10+ books per hour.* Achievable (just) if you are using downloaded records from another database for everything and the materials you are dealing with are not difficult to catalogue, but it doesn't leave you any time for editing mistakes in the records, especially if you are expected to assign shelf locations to each item as you are going along. Not recommended unless it is the only way of getting materials recorded on the catalogue and/or the users of the information service do not require detailed subject access to each item.

Morris's (1992) figures for cataloguing speeds at Iowa State University Library were 3 titles per hour for copy cataloguing,

1 title per hour for recataloguing and 1 title per 60–90 minutes for original cataloguing.

Appropriate levels of staffing

Understaffing:
"What's that, Mr. Mop? Put it under
'History'? I don't know. What do
you think, Mrs. Balloon?"

Sadly, modern organisations are more likely to be understaffed than overstaffed. This is particularly true of information services, and when the pressure is particularly high, public services usually take priority over cataloguing on the grounds that it is more important to have someone at the information desk available to answer inquiries than to have someone working in a back room updating the catalogue. It is therefore unlikely that you will find yourself in the position of having too many cataloguers for the work available.

Consider the example of Tony Tightwad, county librarian for Nowhereshire, who has the task of allocating resources to the Much Gossip public library. When working out how many cataloguers he needs he will consider the following questions:

■ How many new acquisitions does the library handle in an average year?

- How difficult are they to catalogue? (Are they all newly published books/periodicals with ready-made records available for download, weird and wonderful objects which no one has ever catalogued before, or a mixture of the two?)

- How experienced is the cataloguer?

- What level of detail is required in the catalogue record? Is it the same for all materials, or are documents in certain categories to be catalogued in more detail than others?

- How much time is needed for maintaining and/or upgrading the catalogue?

If we know the answers to all these questions, we can refer back to the rough guide to cataloguing speeds in the previous section to calculate the amount of time needed to catalogue an average year's acquisitions. In an ideal world, Tony Tightwad would then realise that Patrick (the long-suffering cataloguer) has more work than he can realistically get through in a year and decides to hire another person to help him. Sadly, it is more likely that Patrick will be told to get on with the job as best he can because there is no money to hire a new member of staff, but if he's lucky he might get Doris the library assistant to help with the bibliographic description.

If you have more than one cataloguer and are dividing up the work between them, you will need to assess the difficulty of the work they are doing individually in order to set realistic targets. It would not, for example, be appropriate to expect a new recruit to achieve the same targets as the most experienced cataloguer in the department (at least, not until their second week in the job!) or to ask someone who is doing mostly original cataloguing to do as many documents in a month as someone else who is mostly editing records downloaded from another database.

Going back to our example, if Tony has a team of library assistants and paraprofessionals working on bibliographic description and information professionals doing subject cataloguing and record checking, he should ideally aim for a ratio of one library assistant per professional cataloguer as the two processes take about the same amount of time, once everyone is fully trained and confident in their work.

Organising time

Back at the coalface, most cataloguers work under pressure – both from the administrators to get as many items done in a day as possible in order to reduce costs, and from the users to get new acquisitions onto the shelf as quickly as possible. The temptation is to sacrifice detail and accuracy – to skimp on the time needed to understand the subject of the document properly, or to abandon authority control and use whatever name and subject terms seem appropriate without investigating what has been used before and whether it is the best way to describe that subject/person/organisation.

Here are a few suggestions on how to organise your work.

Simplify

Review what you are doing regularly and streamline it if possible – if there is a better or more efficient way of doing something, change your working practice.

Sort

Organise your cataloguing into batches of similar materials; if you do a batch of videos, then a batch of books, then a batch of computer software, you will work through the materials faster than you would if you were picking them off the shelf at random because you won't need to stop and think every time you switch to a different format 'what fields do I need to put in this record?' Similarly, if you are cataloguing a variety of different subjects you may find it helpful to 'batch' your work according to subject because you won't need to consult your reference books or lists of subject terms to find the right way to describe the item in hand if you've already catalogued five things on the same subject.

Bite the bullet!

Set aside a regular time every week to deal with problems. If you don't you may find unappealing materials sit and gather dust on your cataloguing shelf for months, and the longer you look at them the more difficult they seem. If they have been sitting on your shelf for longer than a week, they *cannot possibly* be as difficult to catalogue as you think they are! Deal with them, get them out on the shelves and stop worrying about them.

Banish the backlog!

If you have a large backlog to work through which has been waiting to be dealt with for more than a year, check with colleagues whether the items are still required. In a previous job, I inherited a huge backlog of uncatalogued materials (one whole wall of a fairly large office, entirely covered with shelves which were filled with cataloguing backlog). By the time I had been through the shelves and taken out unwanted duplicates and items which were no longer required (some of them had been languishing for years) the backlog had been reduced by about a third. There was still a lot of work to do, but at least it was not *unnecessary* work.

What comes first?

If you have a lot of recataloguing of existing library materials and/or a large backlog to deal with as well as keeping up with new acquisitions, you will probably find it helps to deal with the recataloguing and the backlog as separate projects and to set aside time to work on them every week. The danger otherwise is that you will either neglect your new cataloguing (which needs to continue if you are not to generate yet another backlog) or forget about the project work in the rush to do the more urgent new acquisitions.

Life outside cataloguing

Remember to allow time for attending meetings, training, and catalogue maintenance when calculating how much work you can get through in an average month.

Relax!

Reward yourself (and, if there is more than one of you, your colleagues) for good work. Go out for a drink at the end of the month to celebrate reaching your cataloguing targets, or buy some biscuits to have at your coffee break. It is not so easy to find appropriate times to celebrate good performance in an ongoing job like cataloguing as it is in a project which has definite milestones and a beginning, middle and end, but it is just as important to remind yourself occasionally that you are doing a good job!

Rewards of Cataloguing:
"You have catalogued well. I shall not
kill you today."

4

How to catalogue... and not reinvent the wheel

"File it under 'M'"

It may seem like a mammoth task...

Now we come to the lengthy technical bit – the things you need to consider when setting up an automated catalogue. It may seem like a mammoth task, but it is not necessary to do it in a vacuum; you can benefit from the knowledge and experience of others who have done similar jobs before. There will be a certain amount of unavoidable jargon in this chapter, partly because it is the most concise way of talking about systems and standards, and partly because you will need to learn the jargon in order to communicate with the specialists.

If you are working in a large library, you will probably not be expected to order new computer systems and/or organise major changes in cataloguing procedures until you are a head cataloguer like Hermione Hawkeye. On the other hand, it is possible that you will have the opportunity to work as part of the system replacement project team or help in training others when the cataloguing standards are changed, and if you work in a small library, with only a handful of colleagues (or none) you are likely to find yourself dealing with these questions sooner than you think.

We shall be considering the following:

- how to choose a computer system: what types are currently available and what to ask for;
- internationally accepted cataloguing standards;
- subject access to records: how to provide it;
- maintaining consistency in your catalogue: authority control and why you need it.

What computer software is
being used...?

What you can do with your catalogue will be determined by a number of factors, including:

1. What computer software is being used?

2. How many documents/objects need to be catalogued?

3. What standard (basic, advanced or Rolls-Royce) are they to be catalogued to?

4. What do the users of the information service need to know in order to use the service effectively?

5. How much money is there in the budget? (Answer – Probably not enough for what you want to do!)

It is not very likely, unless you are setting up a new library or automating a card catalogue, that you will have to deal with all of these questions at once. However, systems are regularly upgraded and a migration to a new system is a good opportunity to review and if necessary revise your cataloguing policies. After all, if you want to change from one data format to another and are going to pay anyway to have your data cleaned up and moved to a new system, you might as well pay a little extra and have it converted to the new format in the process.

Choosing a records management system

Buying a computer system is rather like buying a second-hand car: unless you are lucky enough to be an expert yourself, you are pretty much at the mercy of the salesperson. I am not a Great Expert myself, and even if I was, telling you which the best systems are now is not going to be much use to you in six months' or several years' time when you read this. However, here are a few suggestions on what to look for and what questions to ask.

Let's start with a few definitions. In this section, I will normally be using the word 'system' to mean software rather than hardware. If you are buying a completely new system, the best way to go about it is to look for the software which meets your needs and then find some hardware which is capable of running it. If you are not starting from scratch, you presumably already have some hardware and you want to find software which can run on what you've got. Either way, choosing the software for the database is likely to involve more soul-searching than getting the hardware, and even if you are not an expert on how computer systems work, you are an expert on what you want to do with the system under consideration. The final choice may well be out of your hands, unless you are the only person in a position to judge the effectiveness of the systems on offer and there is enough money in the kitty to buy any system you want. Nevertheless, if the system is about to be replaced you should make your requirements known to whoever is in charge of choosing the new one. You may not get what you want, but at least no one will be able to say that you didn't ask for it.

Software/hardware incompatability

There are two basic types of system in use:

- *Integrated library systems* provide all the data management functions required by a library. They track the circulation of library materials, reservations, inter-library loans, acquisitions and any other transactions required as well as handling cataloguing, authority control and database management. They are used by academic and public libraries, and some large to medium-sized special libraries. Integrated systems suitable for small libraries (e.g. school libraries or small corporate libraries) are also available.

- *Database programs* are used when all that is required is a catalogue of available resources. This might be either because the library materials are for reference only and never leave the library, or because they are all available in electronic format, in which case the catalogue record would provide a link to the actual resource. In either case, there would be no need to track the whereabouts of each item in the catalogue. The chosen program might be one designed specifically for use in libraries and information services, or a more general one such as Microsoft Access or Lotus Notes. This is the most common type of system in use by 'virtual' libraries (libraries of electronic resources) and knowledge managers. This type is also used by very small libraries where, if materials are circulated, loans are recorded either manually or in a separate electronic file which does not interact with the catalogue.

Integrated library systems:
"System detects overdue book
in sector 4. Deal with it."

There are three basic types of user interface:

- *Command-driven* programs require the user to type in commands to tell the system what to do. They are quick to use once the commands have been mastered, but learning the commands for a new program is quite time-consuming and frequently frustrating.

- *Menu-driven* programs require you to select options from a menu. This may be done either by typing in the number or initial letter of the option you want or (more frequently) by pointing the mouse and clicking on the required option. This interface is easy to use, but once the program has been learned it can be annoying to have to scroll through menus instead of going straight to the command you want.

- *Forms* are used to present complicated operations (such as, for example, creating a new bibliographic record) in a way which is clear to the user. The screen shows a set of labelled boxes for inputting data, usually with menus at the top and/or bottom of the screen as well.

Most modern computer systems use all three approaches as appropriate, so in most situations the user is able to choose between using menus and using commands. You should be looking for a system which allows you to do as much as possible through the keyboard – when inputting data, having to stop and reach for the mouse to give the next command to the system slows you down considerably.

Command driven programs:
"WORK! Damn you!"

As a cataloguer, you will be interested in how the system handles three things:

- the creation and maintenance of bibliographic records;
- authority control and keyword indexing;
- searching on the online public catalogue.

You will need the following information:

- How many records are already on the database/in the card catalogue?
- On average, how many are added each year?
- How many transactions does the system handle in an average week/day/hour? (NB. If you have never automated your catalogue before, estimating the number of inquiries will be very difficult because they will increase dramatically as soon as there are enough records on the OPAC to make

it worth using. Take the highest estimate for use of the card catalogue and multiply by ten. This will probably still be an underestimate.)

- What cataloguing/coding standards does the library use (or want to use)?

- How many different formats of document (e.g. text, video, electronic resource...) are required?

- How many different fields are needed?

How much of your system is configured
to suit local standards...?

You will probably want to ask the following questions of the vendor:

- How much of the system can be configured to suit your local requirements? For example, is it possible to customise the menus in the OPAC so that your users can find their way around the search options easily?

- Can it 'talk' to other systems – in other words, how easy is it to download and convert data from another source?

- Is there an absolute limit on the number of characters per field? This is a very important question; for example,

Microsoft Access does not allow the creation of fields with a length of more than 255 characters, including spaces. This sounds like a lot, but is inadequate for describing many library documents. It would be virtually impossible to include abstracts in the catalogue record; and any titles longer than 255 characters would have to be abbreviated. A good library system should have no limit on the length of fields – unless you want to set one yourself.

- How is authority control handled? Is the authority file checked automatically every time a new bibliographic record is added to the system and the cataloguer alerted if it contains non-authorised headings? Is it possible to update catalogue records with incorrect headings automatically, by editing the authority record for that heading (this is called 'global editing')? If you put cross-references between different headings into the authority records, will the cross-references appear in the public catalogue? A good system will be able to do all of these – if the one you are considering can't, how are you going to do all these things and how much extra time is it going to take?

- How much does it cost to maintain?

- How much will it cost to move your data to the new system?

You will also want to know how easy the system is to use, how reliable it is, whether there are any bugs in it which prevent it from working as you would wish and how good the technical support for it is. These are questions which everyone in your organisation should be interested in, not just the cataloguers! You could ask the vendor, but you are more likely to get a useful answer if you can find other organisations comparable to your own which have bought the system you are considering and ask them.

International cataloguing standards

The rules, then, tell us what information to enter in a MARC record and where to find the information on our item, and the order in which to enter the information, and even the punctuation that we should use for entering that information. However, we must then turn to the coding manuals for instructions on how to put all that information in a MARC record. (Fritz, 1998)

International cataloguing standards: "Yes, yes I know. 120 different categories of snow."

There are a number of different standards available to choose from. I have chosen to describe only the most important ones currently in use in the English-speaking world, on the grounds that these are the ones you are most likely to encounter in your career. They may be divided into two main categories, as the above quotation makes clear: rules for cataloguing and coding standards which convert the raw data of the catalogue record into something which a computer can interpret. The most widely used standards in libraries are AACR and MARC, but others are gaining in popularity, notably the Dublin Core metadata standard and XML, which may eventually replace MARC as the most common coding standard. Whichever standards you choose to adopt, you should be aware that they are likely to change over time; if you wish to benefit from having a standardised format for your catalogue which allows you to 'talk' to other catalogues (and download their records) you will have to reformat your data periodically. For example, the British Library has stopped developing UKMARC, the former version of MARC used in (most) libraries in Britain. From now on, the preferred MARC format is MARC21 (formerly USMARC). This means that the BL can share development costs with the Library of Congress and the National Library of Canada and that libraries on either side of the Atlantic will be able to exchange data even more easily than before. But changing from UKMARC to MARC21 involves a number of costs and quite a lot of work – it is necessary to retrain staff in the new rules and replace all the old manuals, as well as convert the entire database. In the months after the changeover, cataloguing throughput is likely to go down as even the most experienced staff will have to consult the coding manuals more often.

However, the benefits of using a standard which is continually being revised and updated outweigh the drawbacks; if your library chooses not to follow the herd to the new version of the standard, it may not matter for a while, but in ten or twenty years' time it will probably work out more expensive for the following reasons:

- Vendors of systems concentrate on supplying those which support the most common standards. If you don't use a common standard, you can probably still get a system which will run your database – for a price. You won't have as much choice as someone who did bite the bullet and pay for conversion, though.

- Suppliers of bibliographic records will also concentrate on the most commonly used standards. If you are buying some of your catalogue records from elsewhere rather than creating them all in-house, it may still be possible to get records and convert them to your own standard, or to commission records to your requirements. Again, it will be more expensive than it would be if you had taken the plunge and changed over to a more widely recognised standard. You may even find yourself having to create all your records from scratch (refer back to the list of cataloguing speeds in Chapter 3 to get an idea of the effect this will have on your productivity).

- The old version of the standard which you use will not include instructions and/or coding for cataloguing new formats of document which came along after it ceased to be developed. This may or may not be a problem, depending on your circumstances, but if you want to be on the multimedia cutting edge, using a standard which does not tell you how to catalogue DVDs (for example) could cramp your style.

ISBD

The International Standard for Bibliographic Description, as its name implies, lays down rules for the bibliographic description of documents. It is maintained by IFLA, the International Federation of Library Associations and Institutions, and is available through the IFLA website. ISBD includes a number of standards for different document formats, all of them deriving from the General International Standard for Bibliographic Description, or ISBD(G).

ISBD(G) does not offer guidance on the selection of access points or on creating indexes; its purpose is to provide a standardised method for formal bibliographic description. It is not intended to be used directly by cataloguers describing items in libraries. Instead, it is meant to be used as the basis for developing national cataloguing codes by national library organisations. What it does do is define the basic elements of a bibliographic description, the order in which they should appear in the record and the punctuation which should be used to mark the different parts of the description, so that records created using ISBD-derived cataloguing codes may be exchanged internationally.

There are eight data elements, defined as follows:

1. Title and statement of responsibility
2. Edition
3. Material (or type of publication) specific data
4. Publication, distribution, etc.
5. Physical description
6. Series
7. Notes
8. Standard number (if any) and terms of availability.

Most of these terms are self-explanatory. The 'statement of responsibility' is the statement on the title page which identifies the author/s, editor/s, illustrator/s (etc.) of the document. ISBD is concerned with bibliographic description only, so the statement is transcribed as it appears on the title page, even if the author's name as given on the title page is not the same as the usual form of his or her name. Statements of responsibility may also appear as part of the edition or series statements, if the person responsible for revising the edition in hand or editing the series is not the same as the (original) author of the document. Item 3, the material-specific data, is crucial for some types of document – this is where you would enter the scale of a map, for example – and totally irrelevant for others. The standard number for printed documents would be the ISBN or ISSN; videos, DVDs and audio CDs very often have a standard number now as well. Terms of availability might be simply a note of the cost of buying the document (or access to it); a cataloguer working for a corporate library could also include information on who is authorised to access the document if it contains commercially sensitive information, for example.

Our well-used example, *Dentures of Desire*, if described according to ISBD, would look like this:

Title and statement of responsibility	Dentures of desire / by Cynthia Lustgirdle
Publication, distribution, etc.	London: Cursed Powderpuff Press, 2003
Physical description	452 p.: ill.; 23 cm
Series	Pinnacles of passion

Notes	First published in 1926 by the Gargoyle Press
ISBN	132456257123X

For those wishing to go into the matter further, ISBD(G) has been further elaborated by the production of ISBDs for specific types of material; for example, ISBD(A), which deals with the bibliographic description of antiquarian books, or ISBD(E) for electronic documents. It is unlikely that you will come across a library which uses ISBD directly to catalogue its holdings; most libraries use a national cataloguing code derived from it. In any case, ISBD could not be used on its own for anything but a rudimentary catalogue as it gives no guidance on the creation of access points, but the standards for individual formats could be used in conjunction with local guidelines on access points.

AACR

Anglo-American Cataloguing
Rules:
"Under 'I' for Independence!"
"No, no, 'R' for rebellion!"

The Anglo-American Cataloguing Rules have been around for some time. Their ancestry can be traced back to the publication of the first Anglo-American cataloguing code in 1908. Of course, they have been updated since then! The current edition, AACR2R, last revised in 2002, is to be replaced in a few years' time with a third edition, AACR3 (likely to be published in 2005 or 2006).

AACR is divided into two sections. The first, which is based very closely on ISBD, deals with bibliographic description of documents and consists of a chapter giving the general rules followed by chapters expanding these rules for different formats, in the same way that ISBD(G) is elaborated by the ISBDs for different types of document. The second section deals with the selection of access points for browseable name indexes, including copious guidance on how to establish the correct form of an author's name for both personal and corporate authors and how to select the main entry for a document.

Main entry, as noted above in Chapter 2, is a useful concept if you are creating a card index but largely irrelevant in computer catalogues. The main practical reason for retaining it seems to be in order to provide a standardised way of determining where the document should be filed on the library shelf; this is not really a cataloguing issue, of course. Main entry is also used by some computer systems to determine which fields of a catalogue record should be displayed when the record is shown in brief form (e.g. as part of a list of search results), but it would be just as easy to program the system to display title and first (author) name field from the catalogue record. In fact, the AACR committee considered abolishing the rule of main entry as long ago as

1988;[1] it is likely to be discarded entirely, or retained as an option for card catalogues only, in the near future.

Another slightly contentious part of AACR's approach to access points is the 'rule of three'. This limits the number of authors you are allowed to mention for documents with multiple authors. For example, let us imagine that you have the following item to catalogue:

> Boudoirs of passion: a collection of romantic tales / by Cynthia Lustgirdle, Lascivia Smoochbasket, Dorothea Doomworthy and Janine Ashbless; edited by Bertha Bogwort

Under AACR, you are only allowed to make access points for up to three authors. If there are more than three who perform the same function in creating the work in question, then the main entry for the work goes under title: you only make an access point for the first person named on the title page and omit the names of all the others even from the bibliographic description, substituting '... [et al]' to show that there is more to the statement of responsibility than you have included. In this case, you would include Cynthia (because she is the first person named) and also Bertha (because she is the editor, so she is doing a different job and therefore qualifies for inclusion in a different category) but you would leave out all reference to Lascivia, Dorothea and Janine.

The relevant parts of the catalogue record would look something like this:

[Title and statement of responsibility]

Boudoirs of passion: a collection of romantic tales / by Cynthia Lustgirdle ... [et al]; edited by Bertha Bogwort

[Access points]

Boudoirs of passion *[Main entry]*

Lustgirdle, Cynthia

Bogwort, Bertha

It is obvious why this rule was invented in the days of card catalogues, and it does cut down on the amount of work necessary to catalogue documents with multiple authors. However, for the user of the library, it is frustrating to be unable to find all an author's works from the catalogue. In the case of academic authors, alternative services do exist to enable the searcher to compile a complete bibliography which includes papers in journals and conference proceedings as well as books, but for writers of fiction, finding out what anthologies or collaborative works they have contributed to in the absence of a detailed catalogue record is much more difficult. Some libraries which otherwise adhere strictly to AACR have in fact abandoned the 'rule of three' for certain types of material (the British Library has substituted a 'rule of six' for documents being added to the Eighteenth-Century Short Title Catalogue, for example). Others add the missing information in a contents note which is indexed in their database. Either of these approaches would give enhanced access to the document.

Having pointed out some of the drawbacks to using AACR, I should add that I personally have a bias in favour of it, largely because it is the only cataloguing code I have ever been able to read more than three paragraphs of at a time without falling asleep. It includes much valuable advice on how to establish name headings, especially mediaeval and foreign names. If you should ever find yourself cataloguing something completely outré, such as the spirit writings of George Washington, then AACR will tell you how to establish the correct name heading for George Washington's ghost.

Dublin Core

The Dublin Core Metadata Element Set, usually known simply as Dublin Core or DC, was developed to provide a simple standard for information about online resources. The intention was that Dublin Core metadata (basically a catalogue record under another name) could be embedded in the headers for a web document and would be retrievable by web search engines. The general idea was that the creators of web documents would use DC to add metadata to their documents, so it is not necessarily intended for use by a cataloguing expert. The 15 basic Dublin Core elements are a mixture of bibliographic description and access points:

1. Title
2. Creator (e.g. author, illustrator…)
3. Subject
4. Description
5. Publisher
6. Contributor
7. Date
8. Resource type

9. Format (physical extent and medium)

10. Resource identifier (unambiguous reference, e.g. an ISBN)

11. Source (another resource from which the one being catalogued is derived, e.g. the original photograph which was scanned to create the digital image you are cataloguing)

12. Language

13. Relation (version of x, replaced by x, part of x, etc.)

14. Coverage

15. Rights

So, *Dentures of Desire* in Dublin Core format would look something like this:

Title	Dentures of desire
Creator	Cynthia Lustgirdle
Subject	Dentists (Fiction)
Publisher	Cursed Powderpuff Press
Date	2003
Format	Text, 452 p., 23 cm
Identifier	132456257123X

All of these data elements may be qualified, so Dublin Core is not quite so simple as it appears at first glance. Nevertheless, in practice it has proved to be too basic to be used for general library collections and a number of 'application profiles' which expand on the original scheme are being drafted. Some organisations have adopted the 'belt and braces' approach of embedding Dublin Core data in their online electronic resources as well as cataloguing them in the main library catalogue according to AACR. If you are working on a virtual library which contains only electronic resources, or a KM database, you may find Dublin Core is the best standard to adopt for your service.

ONIX

ONIX categories... including weight:
"Let's just class this one as 'Fixture', shall we?"

ONIX (Online Information Exchange) is a standard for encoding data which is being developed primarily as a means of passing information from publishers to Internet booksellers. It was developed jointly by Book Industry Communication in the UK and the Book Industry Study Group in the US, funded by the Association of American Publishers. It is designed to deliver what they term 'rich product information' – in addition to the basic bibliographic data for a given document, an ONIX record may also include reviews, abstracts and summaries, as well as links to images. The first version of it covered only books, but standards for other formats are either in preparation or already released – the draft ONIX standard for serials was released in 2002 and standards for videos and DVDs are in preparation.

Given that it was developed by and for the book trade, it is not surprising that ONIX contains a mixture of familiar (to librarians) and unfamiliar elements. It has the usual suspects:

1. Identifiers (e.g. ISBN)
2. Authors
3. Title
4. Edition
5. Language
6. Subject
7. Audience
8. Descriptions
9. Publisher
10. Dates

Here's our familiar example again, in very basic ONIX format:

ISBN	132456257123X
DistinctiveTitle	Dentures of Desire
Contributor (Author: PersonNameInverted)	Lustgirdle, Cynthia
Publisher Name	Cursed Powderpuff Press
Publication Date	2003
Number of pages	452 p.

Note the subtle difference in the title: ONIX follows the publisher's convention of using title case (capitalising all significant words) for titles, whereas ISBD and other cataloguing codes derived from it use sentence case (which means capitalising proper nouns and initial words only in

English[2]). ONIX also includes a number of additional elements which are of interest to the book trade: the exact dimensions of the document (including weight, which affects carriage costs), availability and promotions (including minimum order numbers, discounts, promotional deals, etc.). On further inspection, even some of the familiar data elements contain unfamiliar data – the author information may contain details of the author's professional position, employer and/or brief biography, for example. Similarly, the subject terms used are the ones current in the book trade, based on an analysis of how subjects are grouped in bookshops; these would not be detailed enough for most libraries.

So far, ONIX has not really made an impact outside the book trade, but it has the potential to develop into a useful standard for data exchange; it has already been mapped to MARC, so libraries which use MARC for their cataloguing can download and convert ONIX records. One day, perhaps all new acquisitions for a library will arrive complete with an ONIX record created by the publisher and all the library cataloguers will need to do is delete the information in the record which is no longer relevant for their purpose (e.g. the information about promotions) and add the shelf location and any subject terms they want in addition to the ones already provided.

Collection Description

This is a very new idea in the library world, though archivists have always been interested in providing information about collections. The purpose of creating a set of collection-level descriptions of materials in your library is to enable users of the catalogue to limit subject searches to those collections which are most likely to contain the type of information they are looking for: useful if you are searching a very large database, and particularly useful if you are searching a 'virtual database' or a group of databases containing records from a number of different libraries or information services. This is now possible using the Z39.50 protocol which allows you to input a single search to look for records in a number of different databases simultaneously. The Research Support Libraries Programme's Nineteenth-century Pamphlets Project resulted in a database of records for pamphlets held by 21 different university libraries in the UK (including Reading). It is not difficult to imagine circumstances in which a researcher might wish to restrict a search of this database to a particular group of library collections.

The set of data elements was originally developed by UKOLN and first used in 2001. It uses slightly different terminology to the other standards named above – the collection description standard is referred to as a schema and the data elements are called data attributes. The general attributes are:

1. Title
2. Identifier
3. Description
4. Strength (subject depth, stock policy – is it a top-notch research collection which is added to regularly, or the sweepings from someone's attic?)
5. Physical characteristics

6.   Language

7.   Type

8.   Access

9.   Accrual (is the collection still being added to or is it closed?)

10. Legal status

11. Custodial history (who looks after it now? who was responsible for it in the past?)

12. Notes

13. Location

Other attributes which have been added to the basic schema include subject, date (for the time period over which the collection was brought together as well as the date range for the actual documents), agent (e.g. the creator, current owner or administrator of the collection) and the relationship between that collection and other materials, including catalogues and indexes for the collection in hand as well as its sub-collections and any other collections of related interest. This is a useful standard to follow if you are faced with a large number of uncatalogued items which can be divided up into discrete collections, as it means you can provide some online information about what you have relatively quickly before going on to catalogue the individual items (the most important ones first, of course!).

As *Dentures of Desire* is a single work and not a collection, let us suppose that the University of Nowhereshire is fortunate enough to have an archive collection relating to Cynthia Lustgirdle:

Title	Lustgirdle archive
Description	Personal papers and working collection of Cynthia Lustgirdle, and memorabilia collected by her daughter
Strength	Cynthia Lustgirdle (writer of romantic fiction) – National collection
Physical desc.	Printed texts, manuscripts, diaries, letters, objects
Language	English, French, Italian
Accrual status	Open, passive, deposit
Location	Main Library, University of Nowhereshire
Subject	Cynthia Lustgirdle
Subject	Romantic fiction
Creator	Cynthia Lustgirdle
Creator	Gillian Smith
Catalogue	University of Nowhereshire OPAC

MARC

Unlike all the preceding standards, which aim to define what data should appear in a record and what order it should appear in, MARC is basically a coding standard. It was first developed in the late 1960s (the MARC standard for serials was released in 1970) to provide a standard format for putting AACR records onto computers, intially to speed up production of catalogue cards.

The different elements in a record are divided into fields and subfields (as opposed to elements and qualified elements). The

MARC format uses numerical identifiers (known as tags) for fields and a subfield marker plus a letter to divide fields into subfields (the subfield marker is normally shown as the dollar sign, though the actual character used for it may be different depending on which computer system you use). As the field tags range from 000 to 999, it would theoretically be possible to have 999 different fields (or elements) in a MARC record. In fact, many of the tags are not used. The data elements for bibliographic records are divided into ten main groups:

000–099   Fixed fields and coded data (ISBNs and ISSNs are entered here)

100–199   Main (author) entry

200–299   Title + statement of responsibility, edition and publication data

300–399   Physical description

400–499   Series

500–599   Notes

600–699   Subject keywords and headings

700–799   Added entries for authors and titles

800–899   Added entries for series

900–999   References and local information

At first glance this looks terrifying, but some of the potential fields have not been developed and in practice most libraries get away with using less than 40 fields. For example, the only field in 300–399 I have ever been obliged to use in over eleven years of cataloguing is 300 (Physical extent of document). A simple UKMARC record for our imaginary book might look something like this:

Fixed field	008		030622$as2003$benoacr pWjf$leng
ISBN	021.00	$a	123456789X
Author	100.10	$a	Lustgirdle, Cynthia
Title	245.10	$a	Dentures of desire $d by Cynthia Lustgirdle
Publication	260.00	$a	London $b Cursed Powderpuff Press $c 2003
Physical ext.	300.00	$a	452 p. $bill. $c 23 cm.
LCSH subject	650.00	$a	DentistslvFiction
Genre	655.00	$a	Romantic fiction

The good thing about MARC is that it has been around for a long time and has been developed to suit the requirements of libraries. It is well adapted to format bibliographic descriptions and access points for a wide range of different types of document. The main problem with it as it stands is that it was developed for a very different online environment, where storage space was at a premium and all computer systems were command-driven. This is obvious if you look at the 008 field, which packs an enormous amount of encoded information about a document into the space of 40 characters, including the date it was published, the format, whether it is illustrated, whether it is intended for a juvenile audience, and so on. This is very impressive – but modern computer systems usually have the same information in a more easily searchable form elsewhere in the record, either in a note in the bibliographic record or attached to the item record in some fashion.

There are many different versions of MARC around, in the same way that there are different cataloguing codes in different countries. The ones you are most likely to encounter in the English-speaking library world are MARC21 (formerly USMARC) and (less likely now) UKMARC. MARC21 includes standards for coding authority and item records as well as bibliographic records. It even includes a standard for coding community information of the type provided by public libraries, which could also be used by corporate libraries for providing information about the parent organisation. UKMARC is currently (in 2003) being provided free of charge via the British Library's website but is no longer being maintained and updated. MARC21, on the other hand, is supported by the national libraries of Britain, Canada and the United States, which are jointly responsible for developing and maintaining the standard.

XML (Extensible Markup Language)

MARC has dominated the library world for more than thirty years, but at last it has a serious challenger for the role of Universal Coding Standard. XML was developed from HTML and SGML as a markup language for the World Wide Web, so it has a more general remit than MARC. However, librarians and information scientists keen to provide more services in the online environment have been developing various applications of XML for use in libraries.

XML is a hypertext markup standard, so it is well adapted to format information for the World Wide Web. If you want to provide a lot of enhancements to your catalogue (pictures of the objects and documents described or tables of contents, for example) XML will make your life a lot easier than it would be if you were trying to do the same thing via MARC. ONIX, Dublin Core and the Collection Description schema all use XML to encode data (in the case of Dublin Core, because the metadata is to be embedded in a web document, there is really no choice in the matter). XML is also good for showing relationships between different records – so, for example, if you want to provide catalogue records for individual chapters in a book or articles in a journal and link them to the catalogue record for the whole book or the journal title, it is quite easy to do.

The big drawback with XML, if you are using a system which requires you to input field names manually, is the length of the tags needed to format the data. For example, if we were to code our imaginary example in XML (using Dublin Core field labels) the result would look something like this:

<dc.title> Dentures of desire </dc.title>

<dc.creator> Cynthia Lustgirdle </dc.creator>

<dc.subject> <LCSH> Dentists (Fiction) </LCSH> </dc.subject>

<dc.publisher> Cursed Powderpuff Press </dc.publisher>

<dc.date> 2003 </dc.date>

<dc.format> Text </dc.format>

<dc.identifier> <ISBN> 123456789X </ISBN> </dc.identifier>

ONIX is moving away from natural-language tags for its coding; the most recent versions use alphanumeric tags for everything except the labels for data element groups. The same data coded as an ONIX record would look something like this:

```
<product>
<a001> 1234568 </a001>
<b004> 132456257123x </b004>
<b012> BB </b012>
<DistinctiveTitle>
<b028> Dentures of Desire </b028>
</DistinctiveTitle>
<contributor>
<b035> A01 </b035>
<b037> Lustgirdle, Cynthia </b037>
</contributor>
<b061> 452 </b061>
<b081> Cursed Powderpuff Press </b081>
<b003> 2003 </b003>
</product>
```

Most systems will allow you to set up templates for cataloguing with the coding already in place, leaving you with the relatively interesting job of inputting the data from the document you are cataloguing. If your system is not capable of doing this and you find yourself having to type the whole record in from scratch, you are likely to make quite a few typing errors which will affect the quality of the catalogue; you may also find your fingers fall off and your brain explodes with boredom after the first hundred records.

MARC or XML?

If you believe Roy Tennant (2002), the most vociferous advocate of XML, only the most hidebound traditionalists can see any reason to continue using MARC:

> The problems with MARC are serious and extensive, which is why a number of us are increasingly convinced that MARC has outlived its usefulness.

Later on in the same article, he states that when he refers to MARC he is 'conflating several interrelated things' and equates AACR with MARC, confidently asserting that the two are so intertwined that AACR should be junked along with MARC. In fact, the two are not identical – MARC was developed to support AACR, not the other way around. MARC also includes standard coding for data elements not covered by AACR, such as subject headings. There are some problems with AACR as well as MARC, but AACR is not dependent on MARC and claiming that it is actually weakens the case for moving to XML, which does not offer any guidance on how to select the data you put into your

XML record, only how to label the different elements of the record. Why should it? It's a coding standard.

A more balanced view is provided by David J. Fiander (2001), who points out that:

> The rigidity and internal irregularities of MARC are beginning to cause problems for catalogers [*sic*] and users ... perhaps it's time to start looking for alternative data formats that provide flexibility for the next forty years. However ... much further research into embedding current thought into practical data structures is required. Current Internet metadata proposals are incomplete, in that they only describe web resources...

MARC21 is likely to be around for some time yet, as it is supported by three national libraries and widely used throughout the English-speaking library world. It is even developing in new directions, and is unique (at the moment) in providing standardised coding for authority records. However, it has two major weaknesses:

- It is used exclusively in libraries, therefore the systems which are available to an organisation using MARC to encode data are going to be fewer and more expensive than those available to an organisation using XML, which is a standard markup language.
- It is quite difficult to show relationships (especially hierarchical relationships) between different records using MARC: there is no standard coding for linking them together.

The big strength of XML is its (relative) cheapness and flexibility. It has been developed for a modern computer environment; if you wish to add images or sound files to catalogue records or append the full electronic text of a document, XML can do this effortlessly, instead of via a rather clumsy add-on, as is the case in MARC. Similarly, as XML is intended as a hypertext markup language, the facility for linking between different bibliographic records and showing the hierarchical relationships between them is built into the language. However, XML does have a few drawbacks:

- It is not yet developed far enough to be useful for anything but electronic libraries and KM databases. Other libraries and information resource centres hold a wide range of documents in different formats which all require slightly different treatment. AACR and MARC have been criticised for being 'too complicated', but this complexity is due to the fact that the world of real documents (as opposed to virtual ones) is complicated. Of course, this is bound to change as XML becomes more widely used in libraries.

- It is not intended exclusively for use in libraries, and there is as yet no widely accepted standard for labelling fields as there is with MARC21: Dublin Core calls authors 'Creators', ONIX has a data element called 'Contributor' and authors are a subset of that. In the future, if data exchange is going to be maintained at its present level of efficiency, we will need a standard set of universal metadata labels which is as widely used as MARC now is.

Subject cataloguing

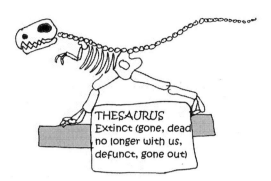

Most general libraries which add subject terms to their catalogue records use Library of Congress Subject Headings, or LCSH. If you download records from elsewhere (from a supplier of bibliographic records or another library), you are likely to find that they come complete with LCSH.

There are two types of controlled subject vocabulary in use in libraries: lists of subject terms and thesauri. A thesaurus, in the special library sense of the term, is a structured list of subject words which shows their relationships with each other, giving references from broader to narrower terms and between related terms. A list of subject words is just what it says: a list of approved terms with no indication of how they relate to each other. Just to confuse things, LCSH is neither one thing nor the other; some groups of terms have been analysed and given thesaurus-style references to show their relationships with each other; many have not. Library of Congress headings may also be subdivided, by date and place as well as by additional subject terms which qualify the first word used (the lead term, as it is usually known), for example:

Murder – Trials – England – York

As you might expect, there are rules governing which subheadings may be used. The exceptions are headings known as 'free-floating' subject headings, which may also be subject headings in their own right:

History

.

.

.

York – History – 18th century

If you are working in a specialised library which covers one or two subjects in depth, you may find that a general subject scheme like LCSH is inadequate for your purpose. If this is the case, you have three options:

1. Use LCSH (or a similar general scheme) despite its inadequacies, subdividing the subject headings as much as possible to give the maximum amount of detail the scheme will allow. This is probably the cheapest option if you are using downloaded records rather than creating your own from scratch and the majority of records come with ready-made subject headings.

2. Find a specialist thesaurus which deals only with your subject. This is easier for some subjects than it is for others; for example, medical libraries have the option of

using Medical Subject Headings (MeSH) which are used by the (US) National Library of Medicine and which may even be present in downloaded records. Libraries dealing with other subjects may have to search around to find a suitable thesaurus. A good starting point is to look at a CD-Rom or online service providing abstracts of articles in your specialist subject to see if they have a thesaurus of controlled subject terms, or to check on the Web for any online thesauri. When you have found something which might be suitable, remember to check how good it is (by consulting your local subject experts, if you don't know enough about the subject to judge for yourself) and how reliable the source is before rushing off to edit all your library records. Not all the thesauri available on the Web are as authoritative as the Getty Institute's Art and Architecture Thesaurus.

3. Create your own thesaurus. This is likely to be the preferred option if you are creating a database for knowledge management; the advantage is that you can provide subject access to your documents which is perfectly tailored to local needs and which can be updated whenever you consider it necessary, without the bureaucracy and delays associated with trying to get the Library of Congress (for example) to accept a new subject term or replace an outdated one. The drawback is that it will take a lot of time and effort to get right, time which you may not have to spare from your other duties.

A good introduction to thesaurus construction, if you wish to go into the matter further, is provided by Aitchison, Gilchrist and Bawden (2000). Just to get an idea of the process, let's imagine that Patrick (our long-suffering cataloguer from Chapter 3) is working on a simple thesaurus for the Much Gossip children's library. He has a list of subject terms under the general heading of 'Transport' and wants to organise them. There are two ways he could go about it. The traditional way is to put them into a 'subject tree' showing the hierarchical relationships, rather like Figure 4.1.

Figure 4.1 **Subject tree: Transport**

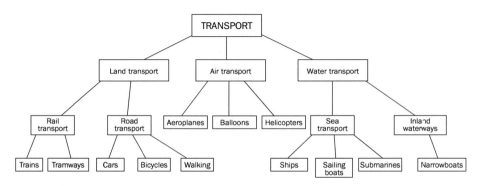

Another way of organising the same information is to draw a 'mental map' of the subject, starting with the main subject term in the middle and grouping the other terms around it (see Figure 4.2). As you see, you end up with something that looks rather like a spiderweb, but many people find this type of diagram easier to work out than the 'subject tree' kind. You may of course find it helpful to do both, and perhaps redo them several times as you work out new relationships between subjects. Eventually, you will be able to reduce your diagrams to an alphabetical list with references between broader and narrower terms and related terms (BT, NT, RT respectively), thus:

Figure 4.2 **Mental map: Transport**

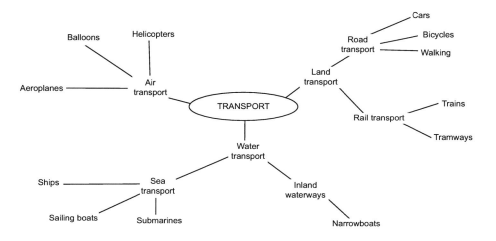

Aeroplanes

> BT   Air transport
>
> RT   Balloons
>
> RT   Helicopters

Air transport

> BT   Transport
>
> NT   Aeroplanes
>
> NT   Balloons
>
> NT   Helicopters
>
> RT   Land transport
>
> RT   Water transport

Balloons
>   BT   Air transport
>   RT   Aeroplanes
>   RT   Helicopters

Bicycles
>   BT   Road transport
>   RT   Cars
>   RT   Walking

Canal transport
>   BT   Water transport
>   NT   Narrowboats

and so on.

Once you have the subject tree and/or the mental map worked out, generating the alphabetical list is relatively easy: of course, if I were doing this for real the thesaurus would include far more terms and look much more complicated. For example, I might want to include terms relating to transport infrastructure (roads and railways: air and sea ports...) as well as those relating to modes of transport, and then I would have the problem of how to integrate them into the tree. I might want to change the subject terms I use to make them more accessible to the target audience ('transport' is not a word you hear the average four-year-old using very often). I might want to link terms from this tree to related terms from another tree (let's say one on 'The sea'). If you are working on an advanced thesaurus for your subject, the time and effort involved will be considerable.

Of course, you can avoid all of this mental effort by not using a controlled vocabulary at all. If you choose this option, the way to provide subject access is simply to take the most significant subject words from the document itself. This is quicker than agonising over which approved term is appropriate for the particular item you are cataloguing, but as I have already pointed out it will ultimately cause problems for users of the catalogue because documents on the same subject will not necessarily all be described in the same words.

"X marks the spot, me hearties! Start digging!"

Authority control

This job is all about ensuring consistency in the access points provided by the catalogue. The most obvious part of it is making sure that all the people adding data to the catalogue are using subject headings and creating name headings in the same way. In the computer age, it is also important to keep tabs on typing errors in the database, as mistyped keywords will not be retrieved in a normal (or at least, correctly spelled) keyword search. A list of the most common typing errors found in library databases is provided online[3] for the edification and amusement of head cataloguers, ranked in order of probability: the most common mistakes are missing out letters (administraton instead of administration) and adding extra ones in words with double letter clusters (recommmendation instead of recommendation, for example). If you are lucky enough to have a system which allows you to do 'search and replace' operations on all records in the database, keeping the most obvious errors at bay is fairly easy, provided that you are sure the word in question has not been deliberately misspelled. If you are not sure, then unfortunately there is no alternative to checking each record individually.

Anglo-American spelling differences are the cause of another minefield here; under the standard rules of bibliographic description, words must be spelled in the bibliographic record as they appear on the actual document (though you may add an extra entry or a note giving the 'correct' spelling if you wish). So, for example, the correct spelling for the title of this book in American English would be:

> Cataloging without tears: managing knowledge in the information society

However, the correct title (assuming no one brings out an American edition with the title 'translated' into American English), in the US as in the UK, is:

> Cataloguing without tears: managing knowledge in the information society

Note the subtle difference in one significant word of the title: a human reading the two titles side by side would usually have to look twice to see the difference, but computers are sticklers for precision. A normal library system, if you input a title search for all records containing the keyword 'cataloging', would not retrieve the (correct) title of this book.

Most systems will allow you to put a 'wild card' character to show that you are unsure of the spelling of a word, or to truncate a word when you want to retrieve all the possible variations of it:

organi?ing	will retrieve organizing and organising
catalog*	will retrieve catalog, catalogue, cataloging, cataloguing...

This is not usually something which the average library user would think of trying when the first search failed. What is needed is a library system with an intelligent search module, which will automatically search for alternative spellings of the words input and present results in several different sets, ranked according to how closely they match the search as input: it is technically possible, but many if not most library catalogues are not programmed to do this.

As well as keeping an eye on typing errors in your database, you will need to make sure that access points for names and subjects are consistent. There are a number of different categories of heading, and you will probably need to use different sources of information to establish consistent rules for each category. They are:

1. Names of people

2. Names of organisations – also known as 'corporate names': companies, schools, pop groups, football teams and conferences may all be treated as corporate entities

3. Names of places – 'geographical names'

4. Titles (usually series titles)

5. Names as subjects: personal, corporate and geographical names

6. Titles as subjects (e.g. Bible – Criticism and interpretation)

7. 'Topical' subjects (e.g. history, botany, geology, dentists...)

Standard rules for creating name headings are included in AACR, but most people prefer to check a reference source for a ready-established heading and only work out the whole thing themselves when the reference sources do not list the name they are looking for. Your research is most likely to follow this procedure:

1. Check your own catalogue to see if the heading is already there (well, duhh...).

2. Search a national or university library catalogue for that heading.

3. *Names of people.* Check a reference source which is likely to have the name you're looking for, e.g. *Dictionary of National Biography* (general reference work for UK people) or Getty's *Union List of Artists' Names* (website, useful for establishing names and dates for artists and illustrators who do not appear in library catalogues).[4]

4. *Names of companies, organisations, etc.* Look in business directories, company websites and/or lists of voluntary organisations for contemporary organisations; try relevant histories of the industry or country for defunct organisations.

5. *Names of places.* Check a reliable gazetteer or website for the correct geographical name, bearing in mind that names of places may change over time and the name in the document you are cataloguing may not be the currently acceptable name for that place: Eboracum → Jorvik → York, for example. Normal practice is to use the most current form of the placename, referring from earlier forms if necessary; this is not exactly a straightforward process when dealing with English counties, which have changed their boundaries frequently during recorded history; some have been done away with entirely (Westmoreland was absorbed into Cumbria in the 1974 local government reorganisation, for example), some have been created out of nothing and some have even died and been reborn (Rutland was absorbed into Leicestershire in the 1980s and reinstated as a unitary authority in 1997).

6. *Subjects.* Check the thesaurus or subject list which you are using; if you are using subheadings, remember to check that these are being created in accordance with the rules given in the 'subject authority' which you are using.

One problem you are likely to encounter when entering new names into your authority file is that of duplicate or difficult-to-establish names. Ideally, you should have all documents by the same author (or about the same entity) filed under the same access point. This is not as easy as it sounds: if you have an author who has decided to be cited as T. Jones on the title page, how do you distinguish between that T. Jones and the half-dozen other T. Joneses who also wrote documents which are in your library? Similarly, if you have annual reports from two different companies with the same name or a book about a country which no longer exists as a political entity, what do you do? The usual answer to this problem, in the case of names of people or organisations, is to keep adding details to the name heading until you have a clear distinction between it and any others which might be confused with it. For example:

Jones, T. (Terence), 1927–1985
Jones, T. (Terence), 1967–

In some cases, with very common names, you might find that adding the year of birth (and/or death) is not enough to distinguish between two different people and you have to add the exact date:

Jones, T. (Tracy), 16 July 1977–
Jones, T. (Tracy), 27 August 1977–

Of course, finding this information may be difficult or impossible! In the case of companies or other organisations with the same name, it is usually possible to distinguish between them by adding the place where they are based or the location of their head office:

Stamp Collectors' Club (Basingstoke)
Stamp Collectors' Club (Birmingham)

If you want to distinguish between different divisions of the same firm (or other corporate entity) you can add more detail:

Intapress Publishing. Cargo Systems
Intapress Publishing. Hazardous Cargo Bulletin

If there is some doubt over which form of name to use and your system can show cross-references in the public catalogue, you could make a cross-reference between the two forms of name: this is particularly useful for people with compound surnames.

De Saussure, Ferdinand
    see Saussure, Ferdinand de

Going back to our old friend Cynthia Lustgirdle, alert readers of Chapter 2 will have noted that her real name is actually Elizabeth Smith. As she always wrote under her pen name and anyone wanting to find her books would expect to look them up under that, they would be entered in the catalogue under Lustgirdle rather than Smith, but a conscientious cataloguer might wish to add a reference from her real name:

Smith, Elizabeth, 1903–1992
    see Lustgirdle, Cynthia

In the case of geographical names, exactly what you do will depend partly on whether there is an exact modern equivalent of the name you have on the actual document (e.g. Sri Lanka rather than Ceylon) and partly on what solution will be most helpful to users of your library. If you are cataloguing documents for an archaeological institute, for example, it may be more helpful to enter the name in its ancient form (Calleva Atrebatum rather than Silchester, for example).

If you are lucky enough to have a computer system which can edit name and subject headings globally (i.e. search for all the instances of the original heading in the database and replace it with the new version), editing incorrect or outdated headings is relatively quick and easy. If you have to edit each record individually, the process is much more laborious and you may find yourself having to sacrifice consistency in the cause of getting new documents catalogued. The difficulty here is not so much the occasional mistyped record. If you are using someone else's rules, they may decide to change them. For example, LCSH does update its list of preferred terms regularly, adding new terms, replacing outdated and politically incorrect ones (e.g. Negroes → Afro-Americans → African Americans).

Names of places may change over time: Eboracom - Yorvik-York (Grand Old Duke of)

Many libraries do not have the staff time to update records individually and are forced into the compromise of using the new term for newly catalogued items and leaving old records unedited. If you are in this situation, you should keep a note of problem headings against the day when your computer system is upgraded or you have some time on your hands – don't abandon hope entirely! If inconsistent headings are causing problems for users of the catalogue, you may be able to talk your boss into giving you some extra time (or extra staff) for the project of upgrading the catalogue and making it more consistent. If not, then providing a list of the headings which haven't been updated together with the new terms will make you slightly less unpopular with the catalogue users.

Notes

1. See paragraph 0.5 of AACR2R (1988).
2. Some languages have different rules for capitalisation: in German, for example, all nouns are capitalised regardless of whether or not they are proper nouns.
3. *Typographical errors in library databases* by Terry Ballard (accessed 22 June 2003 at *http://faculty.quinnipiac.edu/libraries/tballard/ typoscomplete.html*).
4. See the appendix at the back of the book for full references.

Part 2

The nitty-gritty

5

Is it a book, is it a journal...?

Is it a book? Is it a journal?
"No, it's 'Superman'"

Having considered general questions such as what should go into a catalogue record, who should do the cataloguing and what (if any) standards should be followed, we move on to the more pressing practical problem of exactly how to deal with the weird and wonderful things on your cataloguing shelf. How do you answer the key questions, 'What is this item? What is it about?' for this journal, that video, or this website? This chapter aims to explain how to go about answering the first question; Chapter 6 will deal with the second.

Traditionally, library materials have been divided into print and non-print formats, with printed documents being further divided into monographs (books and pamphlets) and serials (journals, newspapers, magazines...). With the advent of electronic formats and above all the development of the Internet, it has become increasingly difficult to behave as if printed documents are the norm and any other kind of document is a messy aberration which should be hidden in a dark corner and not talked about much. Some libraries have so many non-print documents that they have renamed themselves Multimedia Resource Centres, as being a better description of what they actually have in stock. Others are 'virtual' libraries of electronic documents, with no physical materials of any kind.[1]

The latest way of dividing things up by format is to ignore the physical form the document takes and catalogue it in the same way as other materials with the same bibliographic characteristics. Of course, it will still be necessary to take account of the physical form of the document at some stage when creating a description of it, but the important point is which of the following three categories it falls into.

- *Finite resources (monographs)* – books, pamphlets, films, computer files, posters, objects, CDs… are documents which are either complete in one part or intended to be completed in a finite number of parts. Multi-volume books and multimedia kits are finite resources, so is Cynthia Lustgirdle's teaset (part of the Lustgirdle archive at the University of Nowhereshire).

- *Continuing resources (serials)* – academic journals, magazines, newspapers, periodicals (in whatever format: an online journal or the archives of an Internet discussion group would be a continuing resource, just like *The Times* newspaper). These are intended to be issued in instalments for an indefinite period and usually contain information provided by many different people. Whether or not a continuing resource *actually* continues for any length of time is another matter: a journal which ceases publication after only one or two issues is still considered to be a journal. The important thing is the publisher's intention to provide the resource for an indefinite period of time.

- *Integrating resources* – these are a little more difficult to define because they share characteristics of both the preceding categories. Basically, they are things which look like finite resources but are actually periodically updated – the new material supersedes the original, but the whole thing is not upgraded at once so parts of it remain the same. The classic example is a loose-leaf file of information. Lists of regulations and law manuals[2] are often published in this format, because it is much easier (and cheaper) to change a few pages when an update is required than to issue a whole new manual with only one small change in it. Other examples of integrating resources are databases and websites which are regularly updated.

Distinguishing between formats

"I was just wondering, offhand, whether you kept back-issues of *Rhino-Breeder's Monthly*?"

So, having divided the library stock theoretically into three categories, we move on to catalogue some actual documents and discover that life is not quite as simple in practice as it is in theory because it is not always easy to tell which category a document falls into at first glance.

Here are a few questions you should be asking yourself:

1. Is it clear who the author is? If it is, the chances are that the document is a finite resource, but don't assume that it's a continuing resource if there is no obvious author: there are plenty of books and videos out there without a single author, to say nothing of the posters, educational kits and CDs.

2. Is it an object? If so, you should catalogue it as a finite resource even if it is in several parts (a single cup from Cynthia's teaset is still a finite object, for example, but you would normally treat the teaset itself as a multipart finite resource rather than cataloguing each cup and saucer individually).

3. Are there any clues on the document to show what category the publisher thinks it comes into? For example, journals normally have their issue number and/or issue date (volume 1, issue 4; Autumn 2003...) somewhere on the title page or equivalent (often at the top of the screen in the case of an online journal). Modern (post-1970s) journals and books usually also have an ISSN[3] or ISBN,[4] which gives you an additional clue – but don't rely on it too much, because some publishers give ISSNs to series as well as to journals. So you may come across a document which has an ISSN and an ISBN, and you will have to work out whether it's a book or journal from other evidence.

4. Is there any information elsewhere in your library which might help you decide? For example, does the record for the order show whether the document is going to be updated?

"How strange, you're the third librarian to say you've lost issue 13 of 'Mysteries of the Unexplained'..."

5. And when you've decided – is there any practical reason why you might want to ignore the actual bibliographic category the document falls into and assign it to another? Yearbooks are a good example of a type of document which may be catalogued as a continuing or finite resource. Technically, they are continuing resources (produced at intervals for an indefinite period); but if you only ever have the current yearbook in the library and get rid of all trace of the previous one as soon as the new one arrives, you may prefer to catalogue it as a finite resource because it looks neater that way on the catalogue and causes less confusion among your users. Supplements to journals are another grey area: they aren't part of the main sequence of the journal and they aren't always published regularly. They are usually on a clearly defined subject and it may seem more appropriate to catalogue them as finite

resources and shelve them with books on the same subject – but if you do that, are you going to make life more or less difficult for your users, who may not be able to understand the clues you have scattered about in the record to show the link between the supplement and the journal?

Figure 5.1 Title page of *Drum & IBC Guide*

Figures 5.1 and 5.2 provide an interesting example of a document which might be difficult to categorise. This has quite a lot of conflicting information. At the top of the title page, it is described as the second edition and it's a directory which would usually mean that it's a book, but down at the bottom of the page there is an ISSN, which ought to mean that it's a journal. It has the name of a journal (*Hazardous Cargo Bulletin*) prominently displayed on the title page and there is no author statement (apart from the long list of people involved in producing the directory at the bottom of the contents page).

Figure 5.2   Contents page of the *Drum & IBC Guide*

My own solution, if I were cataloguing this item for a business or academic library, would be to treat it as a finite resource but provide a note to say that it was published as a supplement to *Hazardous Cargo Bulletin* and add a title access point for the name of the journal. I would leave out all the personal names of the editorial staff, since there is no way of knowing which of them (if any) had primary responsibility for compiling the directory. If I were creating a detailed catalogue record I would add access points for Brian Dixon, Martin Castle and Brian Statham and a note explaining that these three people contributed articles to the directory. So the record would look something like this:

[Bibliographic description]

Title	The HCB international drum & IBC guide: the international directory of drum, IBC and other industrial packaging producers: plus equipment and service suppliers
Edition	1999: Second edition
Publisher	London: Intapress Publishing Ltd, 1999, c1998[5]
Format	Text
Size/extent	256 p.; 32 cm
Edition note	Published as a supplement to Hazardous cargo bulletin
Contents	Includes articles on the drum and IBC industry by Brian Dixon, Martin Castle and Brian Statham
ISSN	1367-9341

[Access points, not including subject terms][6]

Title	The HCB international drum & IBC guide
Alternate title[7]	International drum & IBC guide
Journal title	Hazardous cargo bulletin
Author	Dixon, Brian
Author	Castle, Martin
Author	Statham, Brian

There are alternative, equally valid ways of interpreting some of this information. For example, I have ignored the logo for *Hazardous Cargo Bulletin* on the title page, but I might equally well have interpreted it as part of the publication details and treated *Hazardous Cargo Bulletin* as a subdivision of Intapress Publishing Ltd, in which case the publication field would read as follows:

Publication	London: Hazardous Cargo Bulletin, Intapress Publishing Ltd, 1999, c1998

On the other hand, if your library has subscribed to this publication with the intention of keeping all the different editions of it, you might prefer to catalogue it as a continuing resource, which is what it actually is (the British Library catalogue record for it says so, so it must be true). The advantage of this is that you would be able to save time, as one record would do for all the volumes and all you would need to do is add new volumes to the existing record as they arrive (a job for Doris the library assistant, leaving you free to concentrate on more challenging work). You would only need to change the main catalogue record if the title was discontinued or your subscription was cancelled, in which case you would want to add this information to the record so that the catalogue users know that there is no point in asking for the 2003 edition! The disadvantage is that you would lose some of the detail which you can add to a record for a finite resource; for example, it is unlikely that the same three people were commissioned to write articles for all the editions of the *Drum & IBC guide*, so you would not want to add extra information about their contributions to the main record. If you were treating this as a continuing resource, the catalogue record would look something like this:

[Bibliographic description]

Title	The HCB international drum & IBC guide: the international directory of drum, IBC and other industrial packaging producers: plus equipment and service suppliers
Publisher	London: Intapress Publishing Ltd.
Holdings	1999–
Format	Text
Size/extent	32 cm.
Edition note	Published as a supplement to *Hazardous cargo bulletin*
ISSN	1367-9341

[Access points]

Title	HCB international drum & IBC guide[8]
Alternate title	International drum & IBC guide
Journal title	Hazardous cargo bulletin

So, what happens if you have a document with conflicting bibliographic information in different places? Suppose you have a book with one title on the cover and a (slightly) different title on the title page, or a video where the cast list on the box is in a different order to the credits on the actual film – how do you decide which version takes priority?

AACR has the useful concept of the 'chief source of information' for a document and a standard list, in order of preference, of other places to look for bibliographic information. This means that two cataloguers using AACR and working on the same document in different libraries should come up with the same bibliographic description. Even if you do not use AACR, the chief source of information is a valuable concept. Work out a sensible way of determining chief sources of information in documents for your own library (if you are not following AACR, you don't have to stick to the same order, but you might like to look at their solution anyway when considering the possibilities) so that your own work is consistent and any colleagues (or successors) can follow the same procedure.

The AACR order of precedence, all other things being equal, for printed finite resources is:

1. Chief source: title page or equivalents (some publications have the title page information laid out over two or more pages)

2. Cover

3. Caption (title at beginning of text)

4. Colophon (this is information provided by the publisher at the end of the book)

5. Running title

6. Other

There are circumstances in which you would be justified in ignoring the usual order of precedence. If the information in the colophon is more complete than that on the cover, for example, AACR states that you should take your information from the most complete source.

AACR does not always choose a chief source of information which would be obvious to a non-cataloguer: the chief source of information for films, videos and DVDs is the credits on the actual film, not what it says on the container the thing comes in or even the label on the tape/reel/disc. This actually makes sense if you think about it: the company making the film would have taken care to get the credits right (and the cast and crew would have made sure they did!). It does mean that if you are cataloguing a film or TV show (in whatever format) you must watch at least part of it in order to be able to describe it properly, which is the best excuse I know of for watching TV at work. You will also need suitable equipment for playing it, and if you catalogue a lot of videos you should ask for some playback equipment to keep in your office, so that you don't have to wander round the building looking for someone with a spare tape recorder or video machine. I assume that you will have a PC capable of playing DVDs, CDs and CD-Roms; if you don't and you have to catalogue this type of material often, ask for an upgrade.

The order of precedence for sound recordings (audio tapes, CDs, vinyl records, etc.) is slightly different. In this case, the chief source of information is taken to be the object and any labels which are fixed to it – for example, the disc and labels on an LP record. Information from the container or 'accompanying textual material' (e.g. a booklet with the lyrics of the songs on the recording) is taken to be the chief source of information if it supplies a 'collective title' (overall title for the whole thing) and the individual labels don't. Finally (and contrary to the rules for film and video) textual information takes precedence over information taken from the recording itself: probably because of the high risk of mishearing or misinterpreting what is being said (or sung, played...). So if you want to listen to the Beatles in the office, you will have to think of a different excuse.

Asking for an upgrade:
"Mr. Bloggis, your computer has put in a
rather unusual request..."

Let's go through the different parts of the bibliographic description and consider what problems you may encounter with each one.

■ *Title*. Some works have several titles plastered over them in different places; we've already dealt with the question of how to select which one to use in your main description, but you might wish to add access points for variant forms of the title (as I did for the *Drum & IBC Guide* in the example). You may also encounter works which are called one thing on the title page but are more widely known under a different title: this is particularly common with older works. For example, the original title of *Dombey and Son* was *Dealings with the firm of Dombey and son: wholesale, retail, and for exportation*,[9] but if your library is lucky enough to have the original, you would want to add an extra title access point so that users looking up *Dombey and Son* in the index would find the first edition filed with all the subsequent ones. ONIX and AACR both allow you to supply a title by which the work is most commonly known: ONIX calls it a 'Distinctive title' and AACR calls it a 'Uniform title'. In addition, AACR provides instructions for supplying 'Collective titles' for works which do not have an overall title: this is very useful when cataloguing sound recordings.

- *Author*. Working out who the author of a given document is can be extremely difficult. If you're doing a very basic catalogue and it is not immediately obvious, the simplest way of dealing with this problem is just to leave all reference to the author out, possibly adding a note to say that there is no evidence in the document to show who the author is. This is not really a satisfactory approach if you are working on a more detailed catalogue. In that case, you would want to check the document itself very thoroughly and also search the catalogues of other libraries to see if it's been catalogued by someone else who managed to find out more about it than you have. Remember that organisations, companies and countries can be authors as well as individuals.

■ *Edition.* It is sometimes difficult to tell the difference between a genuine new edition of a document and a reprint of an existing one. If you can't find any evidence that it is a new edition it is probably safest to assume it is a reprint (treat reissues of works by a different publisher or in a different format as separate editions, and make a new record).

■ *Publication details.* AACR states that the name of the publisher should be given in the shortest internationally recognisable form in the bibliographic record, unless it is part of the statement of responsibility: so Penguin Books Ltd would normally be referred to as Penguin. Of course, if you are not following AACR you don't have to take any notice of this and could just put down the publication details as they appear on the title page (or whatever equivalent you are using as the chief source of information). Even if you are following AACR, there may be times when you would want to give a longer version of the publisher's name than necessary, for example when cataloguing early printed books or other special collections. If you are shortening the publisher's name, you will have to decide exactly how much of it is window dressing and how much is needed to distinguish the publisher of this particular document from another publisher with a similar name; also whether different divisions of the same firm are important enough to be referred to by their own name rather than simply the name of the parent firm. Similarly, if more than one place of publication is given (many publishers are multinational firms with offices in several different countries) should you include all of them, or the first-named place only, or the location of the head office only, or the location of the office in the country you happen to be in when you are cataloguing the document?

■ *Dates.* We have already encountered a publication with two conflicting dates on the title page (it is actually common practice for yearbooks to be published the year before the one they are intended to cover). Other documents which might have multiple dates include video and DVD releases of films (you have the release date of the film, plus the release date of the video or DVD) and repeat printings of literary texts (where the copyright date is not the same as the publication date, but the text is exactly the same as the original and therefore not a new edition). How much information you put into the record will of course depend on how detailed you want your catalogue to be: again, AACR gives rules for determining which date to use. If there is no date, you have a choice between simply omitting the date, stating that there is none or making one up. (If you are going to guess the date, you should make it clear in the catalogue record that you have supplied the date of publication yourself and perhaps add brief details of how you came to that conclusion.)

■ *Series.* The biggest problem with these is the number of series with the same or similar titles. How do you distinguish between three series, all with the title *Technical Reports* (or something equally uninspiring) issued by three different organisations? The answer is to include the name of the organisation or publisher of the series in the series title. You might also want to include the name of the publisher as part of the series title if it is well known under that title.

- *Standard numbers.* These should be included if present, as they are important pieces of information, but should not be relied on exclusively when looking for matching records because they are not always unique. This is true even of ISBNs, which *are* supposed to be unique.

Something else which you will need to consider when working through your cataloguing is granularity. This may sound like something you would look for in a bag of sugar, but is in fact the new term for what used to be called analytical cataloguing, and the best way to explain it is to give an example. Let's suppose (going back to the Much Gossip public library for a moment) that Patrick the cataloguer is working on the local history collection and comes across a set of Much Gossip parish newsletters dating back to 1895. As they are issued by the same church over an indefinite period of time, they count as a continuing resource, so he makes a single record for the whole set with details of exactly which issues the library has. However, this is not going to be very helpful to local historians as it gives no indication of the contents of each newsletter, and as it is a local publication it is extremely unlikely to have been indexed by anyone else. So Patrick decides to provide extra records linked to the main record for the whole set which give more detail, rather in the same way that an archivist would provide a hierarchy of collection-level records, followed by intermediate-level ones and finally records for individual items. In this case, Patrick adds contents tables for each issue of the newsletter and also creates extra catalogue records for the major articles, which are linked via the contents tables to the main record for the newsletter. So the records would be organised on the system as in Figure 5.3.

Figure 5.3 Hierarchical arrangement of analytical records (granularity is not just about bags of sugar!)

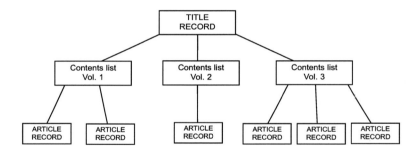

As I explained in Chapter 2, it is only worth going into this sort of detail if you are quite sure that the users of the catalogue need it. If there is a cheaper way of getting at the same information (by subscribing to an indexing service, for example) or if the documents are not likely to be used enough to justify the extra expense of providing a detailed breakdown of the contents, then you would be better employed elsewhere.

The awkward squad: loose-leaf files, websites and skeletons

Let's move on and consider some of the problems specific to different types of document.

Printed documents

In some ways printed documents are much easier to catalogue than anything else, particularly if you are using AACR, because the rules for bibliographic description were made to describe books and adapted for other types of material. However, they do have their moments. There is a much wider variety, both in the quality of the bibliographical information on the document and in the way that it is presented, than in any other format (possibly because printed documents have been around for longer). Documents range from straightforward ones like this book, on clearly defined subjects with well laid out and unambiguous title pages, through the loose-leaf files of integrating resources to the flimsy four-page pamphlet produced by an amateur which has so little information on it that it is necessary to make most of the record up. You may also encounter obscenities such as fascicules[10] – these look like parts of a journal, but are actually parts of a book which is being issued in instalments (sometimes over a very long period of time) by a sadistic publisher who likes to make cataloguers suffer. The simplest way to deal with them is to treat them as continuing resources while they are still being published and finite resources once publication is complete. This does mean cataloguing them at least twice, but the alternative of putting the bits away in a corner and pretending they are not there until the document is complete is not going to make you popular with your users (especially if it's one of those things which takes twenty or thirty years to produce).

Printed music

You may wish to include information such as the key the music is written in and the instruments it is arranged for, as well as the composer (if any), title, publication details, etc. A musician looking for a full orchestral score for *Orpheus in the Underworld* would not be satisfied with a score arranged for voice and piano only, and some pieces of music are only distinguishable from others by the key they are in. If you do not know enough about music to be able to work out this information yourself and there is nothing in the title to indicate what it is, the quickest way to find out is to ask a musician. It is usually possible to work out what instruments a score is arranged for because their names are written down the margin, next to the part they are meant to play, or to check a good music encyclopaedia to find out the key signature of a piece. If you are cataloguing a collection of different pieces (for example, a book of folk songs arranged for voice and piano) rather than a single one, you may want to add a contents list or even (if your library users are likely to want such detail) separate records for each individual piece linked to the main record for the whole document.

Maps

You need to include the scale of the map. Most map publishers thoughtfully include it somewhere on the map; if they don't and there is no way of working it out you should add a note to say that no scale was provided. In some cases you might also want to add the projection (e.g. Mercator) or the coordinates. The other thing you may have to wrestle with here is the title: in order to make the map easily identifiable it may be necessary to treat the series title as part of the main title.

Sound recordings (audio tapes, vinyl records, CDs)

In addition to the usual suspects, you will need to include information about the precise format of the recording and what equipment is needed to play it. Your users may also be interested in knowing how long the recording lasts. This information can only be provided in records for finite resources or analytical records for a continuing resource (e.g. the archive recordings of *The Archers*[11]), so if you want to go into that much detail you need to make a separate record for each unit of information. The rule of 'who is the author' may vary according to the type of material you are cataloguing: for classical music, the composer is considered to be the main author although the conductor (if any) and principal performers of the piece will be given honourable mentions in the catalogue; for popular music, the performers usually get star billing and the composer is less important. The difficulties caused by sound recordings lacking a collective (overall) title have already been noted.

Moving pictures (videos, DVDs, films)

"Hey, I heard they got the exclusive photo rights to the Marquis de Sade's new place..."

We have already discussed the 'chief source of information' for these. As for sound recordings, you will need to indicate what equipment is needed to play the document and any other details which may have an effect on its use – whether or not it is in widescreen format, for example. You will probably need to watch at least the opening credits to get the information you require for the bibliographic description. The 'main author' of a film, according to AACR, is the director; this is logical, given that the director is the person with overall responsibility for shooting and editing the film, but not helpful to the average library user who wants Robert de Niro's latest video release and can't remember the title or who directed it. The main author of a TV series, on the other hand, is usually the scriptwriter or the creator of the original concept, if the series has an identifiable author. In all these cases, even if you were following AACR, you could add a note to say who the principal actors are and make name entries for them in the index.

Graphic materials (postcards, paintings, prints...)

Three potential problems arise here. First, how to identify the method and medium the artist or printer used to create the image – is it a lithograph, a mezzotint, an engraving or something else entirely? Oil painting or acrylic – and what the **** is gouache? If you are going to be cataloguing a lot of these in detail and you don't already have the necessary knowledge to distinguish between different methods of printing and painting, ask for some training. Otherwise, you have three choices: make a wild guess, ask a friendly expert or leave the information out of the record. Which option you take will depend on how important it is in your library to have that information in the catalogue record. Then you have the problem of what to call it. Many graphic images come without titles; if so, you will have to make up a descriptive title. Finally, you may have difficulties identifying the artist. We are not talking about discovering a new Rubens here, but the rather more mundane problem of finding a form of the artist's name which is easily distinguishable from authors with the same name. Artists, printers and photographers will only appear in library catalogues and national name authority lists if they have either written books or are important enough to have books written about them, otherwise you will have to look them up in specialist reference sources such as the Getty Institute's *Union List of Artists' Names*[12] or Plomer's *Dictionaries of the Printers and Booksellers Who Were at Work in England, Scotland and Ireland, 1557–1775* (for early printers).

Objects (skeletons, demon bowls and toys)

There are two important things to remember here. First, you should provide an accurate physical description of the object and, second, bearing in mind what the collection it belongs to is used for, you should provide suitable access points for your users to find it in the catalogue. You may also wish to provide a brief description of what the object is: a demon bowl, for example, is an artefact from ancient Babylon where people believed that evil spirits lurked in the corners of houses and could be trapped underneath bowls with nonsense writing on them, rather in the same way that mice can be trapped in mousetraps. To take a couple of other examples, if you were cataloguing a toy for the Much Gossip toy library you would want to include information on the age range the toy is intended for; if you were cataloguing a skeleton for a medical library which has bits missing from it, you would add that information to the catalogue record so that your medical students will not waste their time (and other people's) asking to see a skeleton which doesn't have the particular bones they have been told to study that week. Difficulties you may encounter include working out the correct way of describing an object (a shallow bowl may also be described as a dish or even a plate) and dating it.

"Personally, I've never had any trouble filing skeletons."

Electronic files, CD-Roms and websites

These may include text, sound, image and movie files. The physical form of the document is not as important as it would be for any of the other categories (although it may be important to know what kind of disk an electronic file is stored on, if it is on a disk or CD-Rom rather than the Internet or company intranet). However, it is vital to include information on what format the file is in, what equipment (hardware and software) is needed to use it and (especially for documents available over the Internet) how big the file is.

Serials (again)

It is vitally important (as I'm sure you realise by now) to include information on which volumes and/or issues of the serial your library holds or (in the case of online resources) has access to. You may occasionally come across serials which have two or more numbering sequences: for example, say the publisher started with volume 1, issue 1 in 1964 and then decided to start a new numbering sequence from volume 1, issue 1 again in 1998. If you have to catalogue something like this, you will need to include the dates of issues as well as their numbers to distinguish between different ones, but you would normally want to include dates anyway. Another (more common) problem with serials is that they sometimes change their title: this creates a dilemma for the cataloguer, who must choose between making a new record for the new title and referring between the records for the serial under its new and old titles, or updating the existing record and noting there that the serial was formerly known under a different title. Which option you choose will depend on how different the new and old titles are.

Notes

1. Unless you count the librarian...
2. The 2002 revision of AACR2 is also published in this format.
3. International Standard Serial Number.
4. International Standard Book Number... but you probably knew that.
5. The copyright date is given as 1998 in very small type at the bottom of the title page. It's not necessary to add this information if you don't want to because the date of publication is taken as 1999 (from the title page and cover); however, it's sometimes useful for the catalogue user to be able to see the copyright date as well as the publication date if these are different.
6. I'll be talking about subject terms in the next chapter.
7. Justified on the grounds that these words are printed much larger than the rest of the title on the title page and cover, and therefore are presumably more significant.
8. MARC allows you to specify the number of 'non-filing characters', i.e. those which should be ignored when constructing the alphabetical index, at the beginning of a title. In the case of this one, the number

of non-filing characters would be 4 (three-letter word 'The' + space). If the coding standard and/or your library system does not allow you to do this, omit any initial words which you don't want in the index – the, a, an... – or give up the idea of having an alphabetical index of titles...

9. Title of the original 1846–1848 edition, published in 20 numbers (19 parts) by Bradbury & Evans, London.

10. Mercifully rare nowadays.

11. For the very few who may not know this is a long-running 'soap opera' on the radio.

12. See the appendix at the back of the book for the full reference.

6

What's a strange attractor? Cataloguing subjects you know nothing about

An indexer's job is to make a detailed analysis of the subject of a document in order to produce an index which will enable the user to locate significant information quickly and efficiently. An abstracter's job is to provide detailed summaries of documents which will help users to decide which are most relevant to their needs and should be read in full. A cataloguer's job is slightly different: the cataloguer is providing a subject index to a whole library (or collection), not just to a single work. This may include providing short summaries of the subject in order to clarify why particular subject terms have been chosen for that document, or even (if your library provides an enhanced catalogue) writing abstracts for each record. However, a cataloguer should not analyse documents to the same level of detail as an indexer would. The purpose of subject cataloguing is to provide an overview of the subject of a given document, not a blow-by-blow account of absolutely everything which the author mentioned in passing. If your users really need the blow-by-blow account, you should be considering providing embedded indexing of electronic copies of the documents *in addition to* the normal catalogue record.

Just to give an example of what I mean, let's suppose that *Dentures of Desire* features a scene in which the heroine meets the Pope. It is not a pivotal scene in the book, which is about the romance between the hero (who is a dentist) and heroine, and so adding a subject reference to show that the Pope makes a cameo appearance in this one chapter is not really necessary and would (in an average library) actually be counter-productive, because users of the catalogue who wanted to find fiction about the Pope would have to look through all the documents which had only a passing reference to him in order to find works where he plays a major part in the story.

On the other hand, the number of subject terms you provide in the catalogue record will vary to some extent, depending on the type of library you are working for. A special or academic library is likely to require a more detailed subject analysis of its documents than a public library would, if only because the needs of the people using the collection are easier to determine. Remember the other key questions from Chapter 1: Who are the library users? What are their information needs? How can the catalogue help them? Good subject cataloguing is an important factor in enabling users to identify and locate the documents they need, when they need them, because it provides *structured* access to the subjects of documents. Natural-language subject access, as provided in title and abstract keyword searching, is a little more haphazard: you have no guarantee that the keywords from the abstract and/or the title have any bearing on the actual subject of the book because they have not passed through the filter of a human brain before being added to the subject index. Of the two keywords in the main title of this book, for example, only one actually describes the subject (cataloguing).

"You're wrong! There is a subject heading for 'gullible'."

Let's take three (imaginary) libraries with very different clienteles and assign subject headings to our non-fiction example from Chapter 2, *Twenty Years Behind the Drill*. The bibliographic description is essentially the same for all three libraries, but as they serve people with very different needs, the subject access points they provide in their catalogues are different.

[Bibliographic description]

Title	Twenty years behind the drill: dentists' reminiscences
Author, etc.	By Alfred Molar, Emily MacCavity, Dent L. Floss and William Amalgam. Edited by G.A. Cranworthy
Edition	Second edition
Publication	London: Minority Interest Press, 2003
Format	Text
ISBN	1456742570239

Size/extent	326 p., illustrated, 18 cm
Language	English

[Name access points]

Editor	Cranworthy, G.A.
Author	Molar, Alfred[1]

The Much Gossip public library does not have the staff time to spend on creating elaborate catalogue entries so confines itself to providing a single subject heading:

Subject (Topic) Dentists (Biography)

By contrast, the University of Nowhereshire runs a highly successful course on dentistry and the cataloguer who dealt with this document decided that it would be appropriate to add extra subject headings to show exactly what each dentist was reminiscing about:

Subject (Topic) Dentists (Biography)

Subject (Topic) Dental hygiene

Subject (Topic) Fillings (Dentistry)

Subject (Topic) Gums – Diseases

Subject (Topic) Teeth – Extraction

The users of the Institute for Dental History, on the other hand, are more interested in the dentists themselves than in the subjects they are talking about:

Subject (Name) Molar, Alfred

Subject (Name) MacCavity, Emily

Subject (Name) Floss, Dent L.

Subject (Name) Amalgam, William

Subject (Topic) Dentists (Biography)

An alternative approach, if you wished to catalogue each chapter or section in more depth, would be to treat each as a distinct unit of information and create separate records for them, linked to an overall record for the whole document. If you find yourself wanting to add more than six subject headings to a record, then you have either over-analysed the subject and should look for broader subject terms or you need to subdivide the document you are cataloguing into smaller units and catalogue those in detail.

Finding the right subject headings

It is not usually necessary to look through the whole document in order to get an idea of what it is about. You will find yourself having to spend more time on this at first and whenever you have to deal with documents in an unfamiliar subject, but you will quickly develop an ability to home in on the important information and define the subject in a few minutes. Here is a checklist to help you get started:

1. Look for a catalogue record from another library (preferably a national library or large academic library like Oxford or Cambridge). Note down the subject headings which they assigned to the book (or download the record onto your system if you don't have one already).

2. Look at the title, publisher's blurb, synopsis and table of contents (if any).

3. Read the preface and/or the conclusion.

4. (If you still haven't got it...) Skim through one or two chapters.

You should end up with a brief description (in not more than six key concepts) of exactly what the document is about. Do not assume, even if you have downloaded a record from a reliable source such as the British Library, that the subject terms they have used are correct and use them without checking them yourself. They were assigned to the document by a human being just like you, and human beings make mistakes. It is also possible, if you have downloaded a record from another catalogue, that you do not use the same subject terms as they do, or that you normally analyse subjects in more depth in your library and want to add extra headings to the record.

Subject headings:
Hunt, dangerous, highly surprising, anachronism...

Once you have your brief description in the same terms as are used in the document itself, you move on to consider how to match this description to the subject terms in use in your library. If you are using uncontrolled vocabulary to describe subjects, you do not actually need to go any further: just put the keywords you have picked out of the document itself straight into the catalogue record. If you are using a controlled subject vocabulary of some kind, you may need to 'translate' the terms used by the author of the document into those approved by the subject thesaurus or listing which you use. Provided that you are using a good thesaurus with clearly worked out relationships between broader and narrower and related terms, together with references from non-preferred terms, this should be quite a simple process and you may find as you are checking your work that there are better headings available which you hadn't thought of using. If you are having difficulties in finding approved terms to convey the subject of the document in hand, try doing a general keyword search (not a subject search) for other catalogue records with the same keywords as you have chosen. You may find other documents on the same or a similar subject have already been catalogued; if so, the subject headings which were assigned to these should give you some clues about what to do with the one you're cataloguing.

It is probably easier to think about this when looking at an example. Figure 6.1 is a thesis on a fairly arcane aspect of chemistry. Following the instructions in the checklist and looking at the title yields the following keywords which look important:

Cadmium sulphide

Cadmium selenide

Metal organic chemical vapour deposition

Figure 6.1 Title page of *A Study of Volatile Precursors for the Growth of Cadmium Sulphide and Cadmium Selenide by Metal Organic Chemical Vapour Deposition*

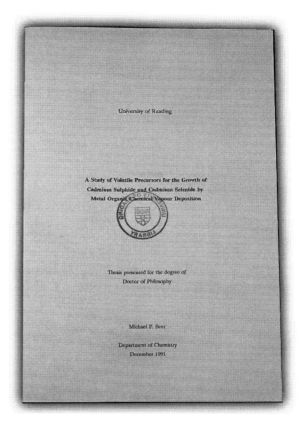

The next step is to check a dictionary of chemistry and/or the subject word list which you are using to find out the answers to the following questions:

1. Are these keywords representative of the subject of the document? In order to answer this question, you may need to check summaries of the work (theses are usually

accompanied by an abstract, for example) and contents lists before looking at a dictionary of the subject to see exactly what the author is talking about. In this case, we find that cadmium sulphide and cadmium selenide are the names of chemicals and metal organic chemical vapour deposition is the name of a chemical process, so these are important keywords for the description of the subject.

2. If you are using a controlled vocabulary such as LCSH, do the terms you have selected require translation into the approved vocabulary? If they do, the thesaurus or subject listing you are using will normally have a reference to the preferred term from the one you have selected.

3. Is it desirable to use these terms to describe the document in the catalogue? For example, if you do not have many works on exactly the same subject, would it be better to use a broader term to describe this one on the grounds that it will be of some interest to the people looking for documents on the broader subject? A controlled vocabulary should refer you to broader, narrower and related terms for the headings you have selected. You may find on reflection that some or all of these are worth adding to the record to enhance access for the users.

In the example, the cataloguer assigning subject headings notes that cadmium selenide, cadmium sulphide and metal organic chemical vapo(u)r deposition are all acceptable under the scheme she is using (LCSH).

Many cataloguers with arts degrees are afraid of scientific and technological documents because they think these subjects are difficult to catalogue. In my experience, the most difficult documents to assign subject headings to are actually social science and humanities works on broad and/or diffuse subjects. Here's an example which I catalogued recently:

[Bibliographic description]

Title	Plato's mistake
Author, etc.	By Richard Church
Publication	London: Allen & Unwin, 1941
Physical desc.	36 p.; 19 cm
Series	P.E.N. books

Plato's Mistake:
"A timeshare? I'll take two!"

This book actually has nothing to do with Plato, despite the title. It is about the role of the poet in modern society, including several would-be humorous asides about how Shelley would have fared if he had been reliant on state sponsorship. I had to read most of the document in order to discover this and then spent about half an hour (this is a long time in cataloguing) trying to find suitable Library of Congress subject headings to convey this. What I ended up with was somewhat less than ideal:

[**Access points**]

Author	Church, Richard
Title	Plato's mistake
Series title	P.E.N. books
Subject	Poetry
Subject	Literature and society
Subject	Literature and state

So do not despair if you are confronted with a pile of documents on some arcane aspect of science which you've never heard of before. Unless the subject is so new that your reference sources haven't caught up with it yet (it can happen) you are likely to find that the authors have defined what they are talking about clearly enough for you to work out the correct subject description without you actually having to try and understand exactly what they're on about. It is not necessary to know exactly what metal organic chemical vapour deposition is in order to assign subject headings to a thesis about it.

As we have seen with the example of *Plato's Mistake*, there could be more traps for the unwary cataloguer in an apparently straightforward document than in one on a subject which you *know* you don't know anything about. If I had assigned subject headings to *Plato's Mistake* purely on the basis of the title page, the catalogue record would have been totally misleading. As it was, the subject headings I eventually assigned were not as good a definition of the content of the document as the ones assigned to *A study of volatile precursors for the growth of cadmium sulphide and cadmium selenide …* were, but on the other hand, trying to define the subject of *Plato's Mistake* was like punching fog.

Splat!

Subject headings:
Jokes, practical

Verifying your information

Having analysed the subject of the document you are cataloguing and assigned subject headings or keywords, the next step is to ensure that you have chosen appropriate terms to describe the document. It will not take very long once you are used to cataloguing this subject – in fact, you will probably be checking the accuracy of your work as you go along – but while you are learning how to do subject cataloguing you may find it helpful to treat the processes of assigning subject headings and checking that they are right for the document you are cataloguing as separate. So, ask yourself the following questions:

1. Have I understood the keywords correctly? This is not such a stupid question as it might seem – some academic disciplines use words which have a totally different meaning in common use, and some words are used in

different ways when describing different subjects. For example, a book entitled *Hedging* could be about gardening, playing the stockmarket or (even) the gentle art of dissimulation. If you are not sure of the correct meaning of a keyword, check a subject dictionary (*not* a general dictionary).

2. Have I translated the keywords from the document into the appropriate terms in use in my library?

3. Have I provided the appropriate level of subject analysis for the catalogue users? Don't forget it is possible to provide too much detail as well as too little.

4. Is there anyone who can check my work? If there is someone else in the organisation with more knowledge of the subject than you who could be asked to provide a second opinion about works you are unsure of, ask them, but remember, if your friendly neighbourhood expert is not a librarian, that *you* are the expert on how the subject headings in the catalogue work and don't let them talk you into using non-approved terms against your better judgement.

"Well, obviously, if we had more than one poisonous book in the library, we'd start a new category..."

Assigning subject and genre headings to fiction

In most libraries, works of fiction (including film, video and DVD as well as texts) do not have subject headings assigned to them. Part of the reason for this is, no doubt, the difficulty in choosing appropriate headings for literary fiction, but most readers do not search the catalogue for fiction on particular topics, preferring to look for works either by author or by genre. Public libraries have generally responded to this demand by putting distinctive labels on the physical document to indicate its genre and (sometimes) shelving genres such as science fiction and detective stories separately from the main run of fiction, without distinguishing these items on the catalogue. The drawback with this, of course, is that if you want to know what genre a particular film or book belongs to it has to be in the library on the shelf. This is not much of a drawback if you are looking for something to read over the weekend, but if you are (for example) a student at the University of Nowhereshire trying to find ten detective stories by different authors in order to write an essay which has to be handed in tomorrow morning and the library interfiles detective stories with other fiction, it can cause problems. In answer to this need, the Library of Congress has produced thesauri of approved genre headings[2] for use in libraries which may be added to catalogue records and used in the same way as ordinary subject headings to identify groups of documents which are not necessarily shelved together in the library.

Genre headings, by definition, are generic and may not provide enough detailed subject access for your users in a special library. If this is the case, you could add ordinary subject headings to the record, either instead of or as well as the genre heading, but if you choose this option in a library which also has non-fiction documents on the same subject you will need to have some way of separating the fiction from the non-fiction. The students at the University of Nowhereshire might be interested to know that a copy of *Dentures of Desire* is available for loan, but it is not going to help them if they are looking for information on careers in dentistry.

The most straightforward way of separating the fiction from the non-fiction is to add a subheading to the records for the fiction titles: the subject index would then file the two categories of document separately. Here's an example from the library catalogue of the University of Nowhereshire, which uses Library of Congress subject headings:

Dentists	(6 titles)
Dentists (Biography)	(16 titles)
Dentists (Drama)	(4 titles)
Dentists (Fiction)	(1 title)
Dentists – Salaries and wages	(24 titles)

If you are cataloguing works of fiction in non-print formats, you also have the option of adding the physical format of the item to the subject heading, as well as having it in the bibliographic description:

Dentists (Fiction) (Videocassettes)

Before embarking on the project of adding subject and/or genre headings to all your fiction, drama and poetry, you may wish to ask yourself the following questions:

1. How easy or difficult is it going to be to assign headings? If your library's holdings of fiction consists entirely of classics (*Moll Flanders*, *Pride and Prejudice*, *The Old Curiosity Shop*, and others of that ilk) and modern literary fiction, it is going to be difficult if not impossible to define the subject and pointless to define the genre.

2. How much difference will it make to your catalogue users? For example, if most of the people who use the library browse the shelves to find what they want, adding extra information to the catalogue may be a waste of time. On the other hand, if they are only browsing the shelves to find what they want because the information they need to select materials is not on the catalogue, adding more information to the catalogue could make a big difference to their lives.

3. How much time have you got to do this? The answer is probably none – so what would you have to stop doing in order to get the extra time to assign headings to fiction?

4. Having considered all the above questions – is it worth it?

Notes

1. Libraries not following AACR's 'rule of three' have the option of adding name headings for the other three authors.
2. These include the *Moving Image Genre-Form Guide*, for assigning genre headings to films and TV shows (Taves et al., 1998).

7

Ici on ne lit pas le français: unknown languages and how to deal with them

"I'm sorry, old chap, but I've absolutely no idea what you're trying to say."

English-speaking people have a reputation (some of it deserved) for being very bad at foreign languages. There is actually no logical reason why an average English speaker should find it more difficult to learn a second language than anyone else; we tend not to bother with other languages because people anxious to communicate with us go to the trouble of learning English. Hold onto that thought when you are given something to catalogue in a language you have never seen before, grit your teeth and give it your best shot. It helps to be able to understand the language of the document you are cataloguing, but it is not absolutely essential. You have quite a lot of knowledge in your head which will help you to work out how to catalogue the thing in front of you, even if you do not know the language it's in:

- You know at least one other language (English) and how it works. You probably also learned a foreign language at school and remember more of it than you think you do.

- You understand how the world works, what's likely to be true and what isn't. A book about fast-breeder nuclear reactors is unlikely to be called *Taking Time to Smell the Flowers*, for example (although you never know nowadays).

- The alphabet you are most familiar with[1] is the most widely used one in the world.

- You have experience of cataloguing similar documents in English, which may help you work out which bits of information on the document are the author, title, place of publication, etc. This is easier with a printed document than anything else (video, CD…) because the layout of title pages and covers tends to follow the same pattern as it would in a British or American book, but experience of cataloguing things in other formats in your own language should help you when faced with another of the same in a different language.

If you are working in a British or American library, the foreign languages you are most likely to encounter are French, German, Spanish and Italian; in Britain, you may also have documents in Welsh, Gaelic or Irish, although strictly speaking these are not 'foreign'! Other languages you may find yourself having to catalogue include Latin, (ancient) Greek and Hebrew (for special collections of Western documents; if cataloguing Eastern documents you are more likely to be meeting Arabic, Persian, Sanskrit and Chinese). Cataloguers working in public libraries which serve areas with a large proportion of black or Asian inhabitants may also find themselves working on Eastern languages, the most common in the UK being Hindi, Urdu, Punjabi, Cantonese and Mandarin Chinese. Other possibilities, particularly if you are working in an academic library, include Japanese, Russian and Arabic.

It may be helpful at this point (before you give up in despair and go off to find an easier job) to consider the relationships between all these languages. It is useful to know how languages are related to each other when trying to understand one you haven't studied: if you don't know a given language but you *have* learned a language related to it you may be able to use what you know about the second language to understand the first. For example, I have found that a knowledge of French and Latin enables me to read Italian, Spanish and Portuguese well enough for cataloguing purposes.

"Me piget, amice alte, sed non comprehendo"

English speakers are off to a good start here. English belongs to the vast group of Indo-European languages, which includes most European languages apart from a few oddball ones like Finnish and Basque.[2] Of the languages already mentioned, Japanese, Cantonese, Mandarin, Arabic and Hebrew belong to different groups: all the others are Indo-European, including Hindi, Urdu and Punjabi. This is interesting, but not necessarily of practical use to the beleaguered cataloguer, because whether or not you can understand what's going on in a language related to one you already know is heavily dependent on how long ago they parted company. The aforementioned group of Indian languages diverged from English a very long time ago, so learning one of them should help you understand the others in the group, but don't expect to be able to sit down and read one of them using only your knowledge of English. Western European languages are a different story: English belongs to the Germanic sub-group of languages, which includes German (obviously), Dutch and Swedish. You can see the family resemblance between German and English if you compare pairs of words:

kommen = [to] come

gehen = [to] go

machen = [to] make

und = and

weiss = white (try saying it with your mouth full)

On the other hand, English includes an enormous number of words with a French origin, thanks to the Norman Conquest and later borrowings, and so a lot of the words in Romance languages (the other large group of Western European languages, all descended from Latin) will look familiar too:

(French)	curieux	information	reproduire
(Spanish)	curioso	información	reproducir
(Italian)	curioso	informazione	riprodurre
(English)	curious	information	[to] reproduce / copy

Portuguese, French, Italian, Spanish and (surprisingly) Romanian are all Romance languages, so if you know one of these you should be able to make a stab at cataloguing materials in the others. If you know one of these and Latin (their ancestor) you are well away.

Of the other European languages you are likely to encounter, Welsh, Irish and Gaelic are all Celtic languages (Irish and Gaelic are more closely related to each other than to Welsh). Russian and Polish are both Slavic languages, though Russian belongs to the East Slavic group and Polish to the West Slavic group, so they are not as closely related as (for example) Spanish and French.

Greek is not especially closely related to any of the other languages mentioned, but a lot of the vocabulary may look familiar because 'learned' words and words for new inventions tend to be borrowed (or constructed) from Latin and/or Greek. Television, for example, is a combination of Greek and Latin words: *tele* (Greek, meaning far away) and *visio* (Latin, via Old French, meaning sight or thing seen).

Non-European languages which you are likely to meet belong to three different groups: Japanese, like Basque, has no close living relatives but is usually included in the Altaic group which also includes Korean, Turkish – and Finnish! Mandarin and Cantonese (Yue) belong to the Sino-Tibetan group. Arabic and Hebrew are Afro-Asiatic languages.

Television, from a combination of Greek and Latin words: "Basically, mate, Callimachus here reckons your vacuum tube's gone..."

So, having had a quick gallop through the main possibilities and how they are related to each other, let's consider the practical problem of what to do when you are confronted with something to catalogue in a foreign language.

What language is it?

Let's start with the basics. I did say earlier that you don't need to understand a language to catalogue documents in it, but you do need to know *what* language it is, because you will probably want to put that information in the catalogue record. So, here goes:

1. Is there anyone you can ask? If it's a new acquisition, find out who ordered it – they ought to know what language it's in. If it's something your library has owned

for a while, check the records and/or the manual catalogue to see if it's been done before.

2. Do you recognise the alphabet or writing system? If not, find out what it is and transliterate it into the Roman alphabet (see the following section for advice on how to do this).

3. Is there a recognisable title page or equivalent? If not, follow the instructions in Chapter 5 to find alternative sources of information. Remember that some writing systems arrange the text differently; Arabic and Hebrew, for example, are written from right to left across the page, not left to right. This means that the title page for a book in Arabic would be found at what we would consider to be the back of the book. Chinese is traditionally written vertically, up and down the page from right to left, and this is the arrangement you will usually find in publications from (for example) Taiwan or Singapore, but anything published in China itself is likely to have been written from left to right across the page. It should be clear from the typographical arrangement (or, failing that, the title page) which method has been used.

4. Can you work out the place of publication? This won't always tell you for sure which language you are looking at, because it doesn't necessarily follow that a document published in (let us say) Germany will be in German and some countries have more than one official language, but it should help you narrow the list of possibilities.

Let's say, for example, that you have a book in a language which at first sight looks like Dutch. You check the place of publication and find that it was published in Pretoria: a brief perusal of a Dutch/English dictionary, followed by a foray on the Web to check an online dictionary, identifies the language as Afrikaans.

Transcribing non-Roman writing systems

Cataloguer wanted for Archaeology collection: strong back and resistance to hernias a must.

I have carefully avoided using the word alphabet in the title for this section because one or two of the languages you may come across do not use alphabets. Chinese, for example, uses ideographs; that is to say, the different symbols in the writing system stand for words or concepts rather than sounds or combinations of sounds. Let's start by looking at something easy: Figure 7.1 shows a rather splendid early eighteenth-century Bible in Hebrew.

As you can see, the printer has helpfully provided a title page in Hebrew and Latin, but the main title is in Hebrew. Standard bibliographic practice requires us to transcribe (convert) the Hebrew into Roman letters. This means that people capable of reading the original Hebrew may have difficulty finding the document in the catalogue if they are not familiar with the library conventions for transliterating the Hebrew alphabet. On the other hand, most Western keyboards are not equipped to input the main title in its original form. Unless you are cataloguing a large collection of documents in this language and your computer systems are already set up to handle non-Roman script (this means programming them to index the different alphabet as well as providing keyboards capable of inputting it) then transliteration is the best way of dealing with this situation. However, in this case, an image of the title page attached to the catalogue record would also be worth providing.

Figure 7.1 Title page of *Biblia Hebraica*

The big problem with non-Roman script is that it is an additional barrier in the way of understanding the document. Transliteration removes the barrier. For example, a word like Τηλεφωνο looks completely alien to someone unfamiliar with the Greek alphabet. Transcribe it into Roman letters and it becomes telephono – a familiar word to most of us.

Non-Roman writing systems:
"Bird... slug, feather... um... bird, beetle, sun... feather... not sure... something..."

For some languages, there may be more than one possible method for converting the original into Roman letters. For example, there are two well-known schemes for transliterating Chinese: they are known as Wade-Giles and Pinying. Pinying has recently replaced Wade-Giles as the favoured scheme in libraries, because it is considered to provide a closer representation of the sounds which native speakers of Chinese actually make when reading the (original) words aloud. Fortunately for our sanity, the Library of Congress website has transliteration tables available for every language you might want (and several you hope you will never encounter) on its website.[3] These are the 'approved' schemes for the library world; if you want to follow the standards in transliteration as in everything else, this is the best source for them.

Understanding the subject

Working out what subject a document is about is basically the same process in a foreign language as it would be in a language you understand well. In other words, you will be using the strategies outlined in Chapter 6 to determine what subject terms to put in the catalogue record. Of course, not knowing the language adds an extra dimension of uncertainty to the process so it will take longer than usual.

The good news for cataloguers of scientific and technical documents is that, once again, they are usually easier to define a subject for than documents on broad, 'arts and humanities' subjects. This is because scientific and technical vocabulary tends to be similar in different languages; for example, the word for telephone is essentially the same in English, German, Dutch, French, Italian, Spanish, Portuguese, Greek, Danish, Polish, Czech and Hungarian.[4] It is not always spelt the same way – telefonja in Hungarian, telefon in Czech, Polish and Danish, and telefono in Italian – but in spite of the variant spellings it is recognisably the same word. This is not as surprising as you might think: the word for telephone has only been in use for just over a hundred years, having been invented at about the same time as the object itself, and most languages borrowed the word from English (the language of the original inventor/s). So newly minted subjects like telecommunications and computer science tend to share vocabulary across languages, whereas long-established subjects like literary criticism and philosophy don't (unless the languages in question are closely related).

Armed with the list of things to look for from Chapter 6, and clutching a dictionary like a talisman,[5] let's look at an example of a book which terrified me at first glance because I don't read Polish (see Figure 7.2).

Figure 7.2 Title page of *Współcześni historycy Brytyjscy*

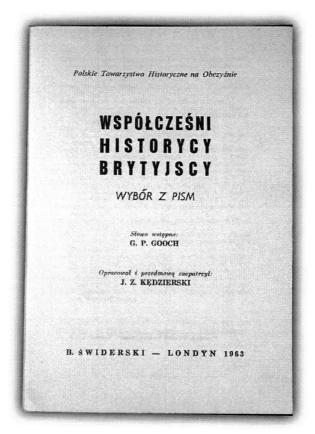

The first job is to sort out what the title is because that may give a clue about the subject of the book. It could be the words across the top of the page, but that looks more like the name of an institution. Checking a list of names reveals that it is indeed the name of a learned Polish institute, so the next bit down is probably the title. It is in larger letters than the name of the institute as well, so that is the most likely candidate. Most of the words are incomprehensible without a dictionary, but two look familiar: historycy and Brytyjscy. This suggests that the book may have something to do with British history, despite the fact that it is in Polish.

At this point I could have got out an English–Polish dictionary and translated the title word for word, but actually I flicked through the book and discovered that it was a collection of essays by British historians, with a short biography of each contributing historian. I did not need to be able to read Polish for this, because the foreword and biographies were in English (see Figure 7.3). This was something of an anti-climax after psyching myself up to do battle with the mysteries of Polish, but one should not look a gift horse in the mouth.[6]

To sum up: when faced with the task of assigning subject terms to a document in a language you are unfamilar with, you should:

1. Check if there are any words in the title, list of contents, publisher's blurb, etc. that look familiar.
2. Look through the book to see if there are any parts of it written in a language you do understand.
3. Look for visual clues – illustrations in books, for example.

Figure 7.3 Foreword of Wspólcześni historycy Brytyjscy

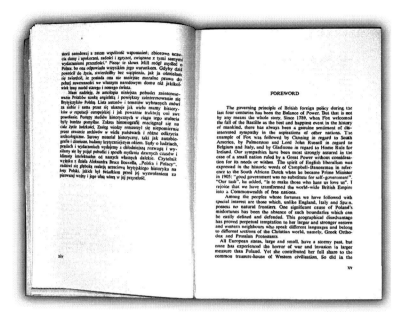

4. Check other catalogues (e.g. the British Library or Library of Congress) to see if it's been catalogued before – but remembering that other cataloguers are not infallible, any more than you are.

5. If at first you don't succede – CHEAT. In other words, see if there is anyone else in the organisation who understands the language better than you do.

6. As a last resort – get a dictionary and translate the title page, cover, publisher's blurb (and as many other things as necessary) word for word, bearing in mind that a word's exact meaning may vary with the context (so you will need to note down the possible meanings of each one

and then work out which is most likely in conjunction with the other words in the title).

Parallel texts, multilingual footnotes and other excitements

Our lives would be a lot simpler if all authors of documents could make up their minds about what language they are going to write in. Of course, most documents are in a single language, but some are in two or more at once. There are several different possibilities:

1. Parallel texts are texts which are printed in two or more languages. They may be printed side by side, page for page, or have the complete text in one language followed by the complete text in the second language. Official publications of the Canadian government are published as parallel texts in English and French. The works of classical authors are also sometimes published as parallel texts, with the Latin or Greek on one page and a translation on the facing page.

2. The main part of the document is in one language, but the preface, footnotes and (sometimes) the title page are in a different language (for example, the eighteenth-century Hebrew Bible encountered earlier has a preface and footnotes in Latin).

3. (Videos, DVDs and films only) The soundtrack is in one language, but subtitles are provided in another language or a selection of other languages.

4. The document is mainly in one language, but includes quotations in other languages.

What you decide to do with the catalogue record will vary according to how much of a given document is in a different language. If you were cataloguing a Canadian official publication, for example, where the whole of the text was supplied in both English and French, you would give the language of the document as 'English and French', perhaps adding a note to say that it is a parallel text, and giving the information from the title page (or title pages) in both languages (ISBD and AACR both include rules for doing this). If you have a text which is mostly in one language, but the preface and notes (and possibly some of the information on the title page) is in a different language, you would probably give the language of the main text as being the language of the whole document but add a note explaining that footnotes etc. are in a different language, but this would of course depend on how extensive the footnotes and preface were in relation to the main text. Going back to our earlier examples, I gave 'Hebrew and Latin' as the languages of the eighteenth-century Hebrew Bible, adding a note to explain that although the actual text of the Bible was all in Hebrew, the preface, commentary and notes were in Latin (and in this case, that meant there was more Latin in the book than Hebrew...). On the other hand, the collection of essays in Polish by British historians was described as being in Polish, with a note to say that the preface and brief biographical details for each historian were in English – most of the book and all of the title page were in Polish, so it would have been misleading to describe the whole thing as being in both languages.

If you are cataloguing a translation of a document, as for example *The Tale of Mrs Tittlemouse* in Afrikaans, it is usually helpful to add the title in the original language to the record as well:

Distinctive/uniform title   The tale of Mrs Tittlemouse

Title   Die verhaal van Mevrou
                                 Trippelmuis

Practical problems

"Says here they believed that if you ever
translated or transcribed their god's name
it was an invitation to demons! Poor
credulous fools!"

Finally, here are a few things to bear in mind when you are beavering away on foreign-language materials:

- *Beware of 'faux amis'.* Just because a word looks familiar, it does not necessarily mean exactly the same in the language you are working on as it would in English. It may not even mean the same as it did last time you encountered it in that language. For example, the French word *mémoire* may mean (a) memory or a memorandum, depending on whether it is feminine or masculine. Just to complicate matters further, the feminine *mémoire* also has several more metaphorical meanings: reputation, good name, renown, fame. So, if your first attempt at working out the meaning of the title or subject of the document doesn't seem to make sense, check all the keywords in a good dictionary to be sure that you have got the meanings right.

■ *Can your system cope with the extra characters?* Many languages have accents or additional letters not found in the standard Roman alphabet. If your system is not set up to deal with an extended character set, you will have to decide what to do: ignore accents and change extra characters into letters which your system can cope with, or agitate for a new font and/or a different system which can cope. If you only have a small collection of foreign-language materials, it is probably not worth trying to get the system changed, but add it to your list of things to ask for next time it's upgraded.

■ *Allow extra time for dealing with audio materials.* These are the most difficult things to catalogue because you do not have any visual clues to help you to understand what is going on (as you would with a film or video) and the language is spoken rather than written – you can't slow it down and you may not be able to work out how to spell words you don't know (so looking things up in a dictionary is not going to be easy).

- *Be aware of cultural differences.* These may lead you to misinterpret the way information is presented. For example, the Chinese (and many other people from the Far East) would normally write their names down with the family name first and their personal name second, whereas Westerners put personal names first and family names second, except when compiling registers and indexes. If you didn't know this and happened to be cataloguing a document by a Chinese author, you might easily get the name the wrong way round.[7]

- *Check your sources carefully.* If you ask someone who knows the language for help, choose someone reliable (not the company buffoon!) and make sure they understand exactly what you want to know. This is especially important if you ask someone else to transliterate a title page for you, because they may not use the same transliteration scheme as you do. If you are using a dictionary to look up words, pick a good one. This is important if you are cataloguing for an academic or special library; pocket dictionaries do not include all possible meanings of every word in the language (if they did, you wouldn't be able to fit them in your pocket) and won't always have the specialised vocabulary which you are trying to translate. For the same reason, it is unwise to rely on computerised translation programs such as the translation service offered on Google: these are programmed to translate words into the most commonly used equivalent in the target language regardless of context. Specialist dictionaries are available for a number of different subjects.

- *Learn the grammar.* If you are cataloguing a lot of documents in a foreign language, it is worth learning some of the grammar (as well as the vocabulary) because it will help you to understand more. This is particularly true of highly inflected languages like Latin. Ask your employer to include it in your on-the-job training: they might say no, but if you don't ask they are unlikely to think of sending you on a language course by themselves.

- *Take a linguistics course.* If you are cataloguing materials in a wide variety of languages, it may be helpful to go on a linguistics course rather than attempting to learn all the languages you are working on. Linguistics is the study of how languages work (as opposed to the study of one particular language). This is precisely the kind of training you need to enable you to catalogue documents in languages you don't know.

- *Have fun!* Think of this as an opportunity to learn about something new rather than a frustration which is getting in the way of doing your Real Job (of putting as many things onto the system as possible in the time allowed). Languages and the different ways they work are fascinating, and you are being paid to find out about a new one. Enjoy the challenge!

Notes

1. If you were looking for the one which had the most users in a single language, the Chinese writing system might win; but the Roman alphabet is the one which is used for the largest number of different languages.
2. Basque is the only European language which has no known living relatives: strange, but true...
3. See the appendix for more details.

4. And probably every other language in the world which has a word for it…

5. Metaphorically, that is: I often use an online dictionary because it's less hassle than going to look in the reference section to see if we have one for the right language.

6. Unless of course the gift tag reads 'To the Trojans, with best wishes from Odysseus'.

7. Just to keep life interesting, some documents by Far Eastern authors do have their name in the 'Western' order – personal name followed by family name – but these are usually documents published in English.

Special cases

The purpose of this chapter is to provide further details on how to catalogue materials in special categories. The categories are not necessarily related to each other; they range from archives and rare books through children's books to the ultra-modern electronic files and websites. What they have in common is that all require you to think about issues other than how to do a bibliographic and subject description of the item you are cataloguing. This might be the actual physical form of the document, as for example the binding of a rare book or the type of paint used to produce an image; the intended and actual audience of the document (is Robinson Crusoe a children's book or not?); or the availability and conditions of use for a website not controlled by your organisation.

Manuscripts, archival collections and rare books

> ...a difference is a difference only if it makes a difference.
> Darrell Huff, *How to Lie with Statistics*

By the time you get a job working on collections like this, you should be a cataloguer with several years' experience. Cataloguing rare books is much like any other kind of cataloguing, with a few extra layers of detail added; cataloguing manuscripts and archives is different, because they are usually unique. If you are working in a library with large numbers of mediaeval manuscripts, you will probably be given extra training in how to deal with them. This section is a quick run through the extra clues you will need to add to the catalogue records for these types of material.

Documents may qualify for special treatment in a number of different ways:

- *rarity* – where there are very few other copies in existence, or none;
- *age* – very old documents will usually qualify under rarity as well;
- *beauty* – for example, a book with an elaborate binding or an illuminated manuscript;
- *part of a special collection* – the document in itself is not particularly rare or interesting but forms part of a collection which is important to researchers (for example, some of the documents in the local history collection at Much Gossip public library);
- *provenance* – where the document has been previously owned by someone famous, or has interesting annotations or inscriptions inside it.

A document may be rare without being particularly old. Figures 8.1 and 8.2 illustrate an example of a modern 'rare book' – only 250 numbered copies were printed, so despite the fact that it was published in 2000 it is actually rarer than some early nineteenth-century titles.

Provenance:
"And this one here belonged to Marie Curie."

Figure 8.1 Title page of *Degrees of Fear*

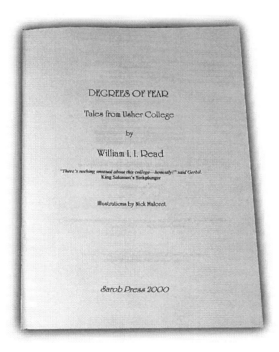

The most important thing to bear in mind when you are cataloguing any collection of this nature is that you are providing information for researchers. They are not like ordinary library users: they are interested not only in the content of the thing you are cataloguing, but in a whole range of different features of it – who made it (e.g. who printed and published it), who owned it before you got your hands on it (the provenance), what it looks like (e.g. the binding, the illustrations) and anything else which marks this particular copy of the work out from other copies in existence. In the case of *Degrees of Fear*, this would include the number of the copy you are cataloguing.

Figure 8.2   Back of title page of *Degrees of Fear*

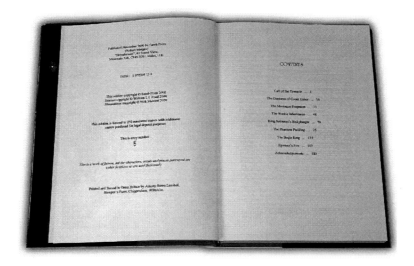

Let's take this book as an example: a volume of seventeenth-century Italian poetry from the Overstone Library at the University of Reading (see Figures 8.3 to 8.5).

Figure 8.3 Title page of *Bacco in Toscana*

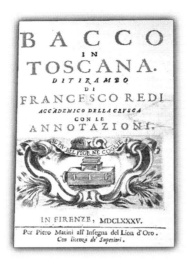

Figure 8.4 Book labels: inside front cover of *Bacco in Toscana*

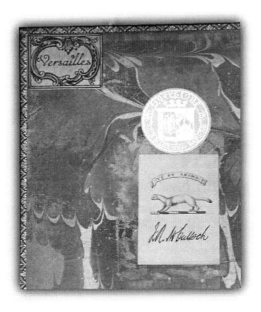

Figure 8.5 Binding of *Bacco in Toscana*, showing armorial stamp of Madame de Pompadour

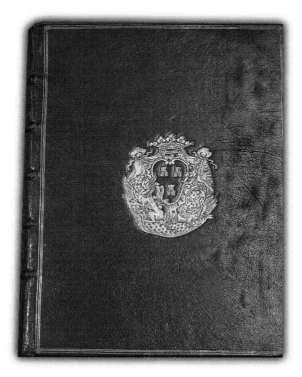

This sends three researchers into ecstasies for completely different reasons. Emily Font, a researcher into printing history, is interested in it because it has several good examples of seventeenth-century type ornaments (decorations added to the page to make it look interesting, such as the vignette on the title page). Arthur Vellum, on the other hand, likes it because it has been given an armorial binding: that is, it has been bound specially for a particular person's library and the arms of that person have been stamped on the cover (which sends two messages: (1) I am stinking rich and (2) I am important enough to have a coat of arms of my own). Finally, Melanie Booksleuth, who is interested in provenance, is sent into ecstasies because this particular book once belonged to Madame de Pompadour, the evidence for this being her arms stamped on the cover and the Versailles label inside, indicating that the book was usually kept at the Palace of Versailles.[1]

If you are cataloguing a collection of very old and/or fragile documents, you will want to provide enough information in the catalogue record to enable a researcher to make an informed choice about whether it is really necessary for them to handle the actual document. This is something you should be aiming for in ordinary cataloguing when you provide a bibliographic description and a set of subject and author access points. But when dealing with special collections, because (as we have seen) researchers are interested in a wider range of features of the document than the average person, the extra information you put into the catalogue will cut down on the number of requests to look at something 'just in case' it's of interest and reduce the amount of wear and tear on the original. If the original is particularly fragile, you might wish to consider providing a digitised image of it, as the British Library have done with their Beowulf manuscript. This would further reduce the number of requests to handle the original, but is a somewhat expensive and time-consuming process; you will need to decide whether the extra work involved in digitising the document is going to be worth it.

A detailed catalogue description serves another purpose: if the worst happens and your Gutenberg Bible or manuscript of *Wuthering Heights* is stolen, the catalogue record will be an invaluable piece of evidence to help you establish ownership of the errant document, if and when it turns up again.

What does all this mean in practical terms? Basically, you are going to have to second-guess not only the Average Library User, who is merely interested in obvious things like the title, author and subject of the document in question, but also the Researcher, who may want to know everything about that particular copy down to the ink blot on page 27, and maybe even Posterity, which in fifty or a hundred years' time will be sneering at your primitive early twenty-first century cataloguing and demanding to know why you didn't put *this* indispensible piece of information into the record. Try not to worry about posterity too much; second-guessing contemporary researchers is quite enough mental effort to be going on with.

"Hello, I'm here to do research for my book 'Unusual Stains on Mediaeval Manuscripts'."

So, we are looking at the ultimate challenge in cataloguing – the Rolls-Royce option with all the trimmings. You will want to add as many enhancements and extra access points as you have time for, and that is where the difficulties begin to arise. Unless you are in the enviable position of having a collection to catalogue and an employer who is happy to allow you to take as long as you think necessary over it,[2] you will be working against the clock just as much as any other cataloguer and you will have to use your judgement to decide what features of a book are important enough to spend a lot of time on. You may also wish to consider, when adding extra detail to records, whether it is going to be helpful in *every* case. For example, when cataloguing special collections at Reading, I would not normally describe bindings of books unless they were particularly beautiful or unusual. Standard library half-bindings or bindings which had undergone extensive repair were not usually described in the catalogue. Of course (staying with the example of binding for the moment), if you are going to adopt this approach, it is necessary to find out what is unusual before you start so that you can make an informed decision about what to put in the catalogue and what to leave out. The purpose of providing extra notes and access points is to enable the catalogue user to pinpoint documents which match the search criteria; so the details you add to the record should use the narrowest possible terms – sprinkled calf or painted calf bindings rather than simply calf bindings, for example. If you don't give a clear enough description then the person wanting to find examples of painted calf bindings from your collections will have to go and look at all 800 books which are described as having calf bindings on the system, which rather defeats the object of putting the information in the catalogue record. Adding pictures of the bindings to the catalogue record is helpful up to a point, but if you do happen to have 800 calf-bound books and you haven't put anything in the catalogue records to divide them into sub-categories where possible, your users will give up in disgust after looking at the first 50 or so pictures and go and look at the actual books instead as being less time-consuming. Images of interesting features of the document you are cataloguing are only helpful to the user if there is some means of picking it out from the crowd of similar materials. For that you need keywords and access points.

The more you know, the better your cataloguing will be. This is true for any kind of cataloguing, but particularly so for rare book and manuscript cataloguing. You will need background information on the following subjects:

History of writing:
"If I were you I'd stick to bison."

1. *History of writing* – including alphabets and writing mediums, how manuscripts were produced, methods of illumination, etc.

2. *History of printing* – technological development of presses, invention of moveable type, development of different methods for colour printing and illustrations, typefaces, important presses and publishers...

3. *Paper manufacture, parchment, etc.* – different materials used for writing or printing on.

4. *Binding techniques* – development of different methods for transforming loose sheets into bound documents. (NB: A knowledge of the history of binding may help when you are trying to work out the date a book was bound.)

5. *Previous history of the collection you are cataloguing* – This is partly so that you can identify the person who has written 'To Gerald with love from Joy' inside the book you are cataloguing, or the authors of letters who identify themselves only by nicknames or surnames, but also because what is important for researchers to know depends on the context of the document. The previous history of the collection is an important part of the context; if you know that Gerald and Joy are the composer Gerald Finzi and his wife Joy, the inscription is going to be slightly more significant to a researcher than one which was written by Joy Bloggs in a book which she gave to her nephew as a Christmas present.

6. *Heraldry* – useful for identifying previous owners where an armorial stamp or bookplate is present. You don't need to become an expert, but you do need to learn enough to be able to recognise a description of the arms on the document you are cataloguing in a dictionary of heraldry.

All of these pieces of information will help you to determine the answers to the following questions:

1. What is important and/or unique about this document?

2. What needs to be added to the catalogue record to provide a useful description of this document *in this context*?

Heraldry: Sir Giles of Bulham Library - Two tomes argent and Spectacles Rampant Sinister on a Field Manilla.

You may find it necessary to provide extra access points relating to physical characteristics of the document – the binding or the typeface, for example. The American Library Association's Association of College and Research Libraries has produced a series of thesauri for this purpose. These are well thought out, and as they have been specifically produced for the purpose of cataloguing rare and antiquarian documents they are considerably more detailed than the equivalent 'approved' terms would be in a more general scheme like LCSH. Thesauri for binding and provenance terms, type, paper and printing and publishing terms are available through the ACRL website (*http://www.ala.org/ACRL/*); they have also produced a thesaurus of genre terms for rare books and special collections.

A sample record with these additional access points might look like this:

[Bibliographic description]

Title	Dentures of desire
Author, etc.	Cynthia Lustgirdle; illustrated by William Rembrandt Robinson
Publication	London: Cursed Powderpuff Press, 2003
Series	Pinnacles of passion
Format	Text
Size/extent	452 p., 23 cm
Illustrations	1 coloured plate (frontispiece)
Language	English
Printer	Printed by Joseph Bloggs
Editions	First published in 1926 by the Gargoyle Press; this edition is limited to 250 copies
Local note	Copy no. 3
Inscriptions etc.	Signed by the author; presented to the library by Gillian Smith in memory of her mother Elizabeth Smith (aka Cynthia Lustgirdle) – RE/U-1
Binding	Publisher's original paper binding – RE/U-1

[Access points]

Author	Lustgirdle, Cynthia
Title	Dentures of desire

Series	Pinnacles of passion
Subject	Dentists (Fiction)
	Romantic fiction
Illustrator	Robinson, William Rembrandt
Publisher	Cursed Powderpuff Press
Previous owner	Smith, Gillian
Binding	Publishers' paper bindings (Binding) – England – London – 21st century – rbbin – RE/U-1
Provenance	Authors' autographs (Provenance) – Great Britain – 21st century – rbprov – RE/U-1
Publishing	Limitation statements (Publishing) – England – London – 21st century – rbpub

Libraries which add copy-specific details to their catalogue for special materials also add an identifier to the end of each copy-specific field (usually the inter-library loan code for their library) to distinguish between information which only applies to their copy and information which is true for all copies of that document. The identifier is usually not displayed in the public catalogue; its main purpose in the record is to highlight the copy-specific information for the benefit of libraries wishing to download that record to their own database and use it as a basis for cataloguing their own copy of the document. In this case, the binding and provenance fields all have the identifier – because there is no guarantee that all the other copies of this book are still in their original binding, or that they have all been signed by the author – but the publishing field does not, because the limitation statement (telling you how many copies were printed) should appear in all the copies of the book. The number of the copy owned by the library is given in a local note.[3] The other piece of hieroglyphics in there is the code for the thesaurus where the term came from: 'rbbin' for binding terms, 'rbprov' for provenance and 'rbpub' for publishing. The name of each thesaurus is also spelled out in full as part of the lead term, under the time-honoured 'belt and braces' system (the codes are not usually displayed in the public catalogue). Again, this is to make data exchange between catalogues easier – a cataloguer from another library who downloads your masterpiece of rare book cataloguing with a view to using it in their own database will need to know where you got your index terms from.

If you have a large collection of documents which need to be catalogued to this standard, it is helpful to have the index terms subdivided in some way. In the example, each of the physical characteristic access points is subdivided by place and date; so a catalogue user looking for twenty-first century limited editions would be able to isolate them from limited editions published in other centuries.

Below are a few things to watch out for.

Dates

Trying to date manuscripts or printed texts which do not have dates on them already is a frustrating process. There are several strategies you can adopt:

1. Check your own library records for information relating to this item. If it has been manually catalogued, check the card catalogue; if you have a printed catalogue or a handlist, check that.

2. Check other library catalogues for any records relating to this title. Do not automatically assume if you find any that they relate to the same edition! Check carefully to see if all other details are the same; if they are, you could put the date in with a question mark. If not, is there any evidence to show whether your edition was published before or after theirs?

"I see you've dated it at 1795. I'd say that makes it a pretty good piece of writing from a man who'd been dead for ten years."

3. Look at the illustrations (if any). What technique was used to produce them? This may give you a date before which the title cannot have been produced; for example, lithography was not invented until the late eighteenth century, so any book illustrated with lithographs cannot have been produced earlier than this. If there are people in the illustrations, how are they dressed? This may help you to estimate the date, or at least the century, when the book was printed, but before blithely going ahead and adding the information to the catalogue record, make

sure the costumes in the illustrations are meant to be contemporary with the people who produced the book. Historical costumes are no help at all!

4. Are there any dated inscriptions inside? If there are inscriptions without dates, do you know when the person who wrote the inscription lived? Again, this will not help you to establish a precise date of publication (unless you are very lucky), but it should give you a rough idea of when the book was produced.

5. What style of binding has been used? You need to treat this question with caution; it may give you a 'last possible' date for the book to have been made, but you need to remember that the text itself could be older than its binding; also (annoyingly) that you may get the date of the binding wrong because the book was deliberately rebound in an archaic style, either in imitation of the previous binding or because the person commissioning the binding thought it more appropriate for that text. However, if you treat this subject with caution and take into account all other factors, dating the binding could help you to work out an approximate date for the title.

6. Has the binding been signed? Some binders stuck labels inside books they bound, or stamped them, either somewhere on the cover or on one of the endpapers (see Figure 8.6). You need to check carefully for binder's stamps as they are quite small and difficult to see, but if you can identify the firm of binders it should help you to date the binding, which in turn may help to date the book.

Figure 8.6 Example of binder's stamp

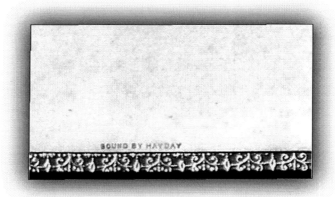

Figures 8.7 and 8.8 show an example of a book without a date: Isaac Watts's *Hymns and Moral Songs*, a popular selection of children's poems with a moral theme. This particular copy lives in the Children's Collection at Reading University Library. It is a good example of a title which can be tentatively dated using information from the book itself. First, we note the illustrations which show people in mid-Victorian costume. Second, we note that Isaac Watts died in 1748, so it is possible for a collection of his poems to have been printed 100 years later. Finally, we find an inscription on the back of the second page which tells us that it was presented to Alfred Heath on his sixth birthday in January 1850.[4] Armed with this information, and assuming that Alfred's Papa bought him a book hot off the presses rather than one which had been languishing in a bookshop for several years, I dated the book to 1849, with a question mark and a note explaining how the date was arrived at.

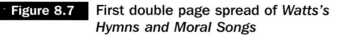

Figure 8.7 First double page spread of *Watts's Hymns and Moral Songs*

Another date-related problem, caused by the French this time, relates to books produced in the twenty years or so after the French Revolution. The Republican government, determined to eradicate all traces of superstition and create a modern, forward-looking society, produced a new calendar with new names for all the months and abandoned Common Era/Anno Domini dates. The revolutionary calendar was adopted in 1793, which became 'an 1' (Year 1). Standard bibliographic practice (and consistency) requires us to convert non-Common Era dates; the problem with doing this to the

French revolutionary calendar dates is that their New Year happened in the autumn, so 'an 1' is actually 1792–1793, 'an 2' is 1793–1794... you get the picture. Without the month of publication as well as the year, it can't be done; so you have to resort to putting '1792 or 1793' in the catalogue record, and hope that everyone will realise that you are not being indecisive just for the sake of it.

Figure 8.8 **Inscription from *Watts's Hymns and Moral Songs***

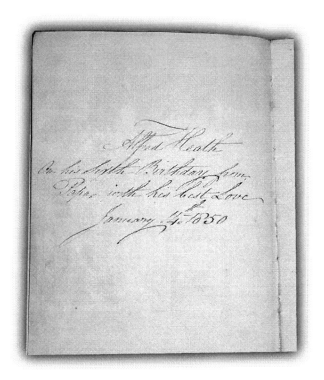

The French Revolution's calendar of 1793, which became Year 1:
"Happy revolutionary birthday! One year old today!"

Manuscripts and archival materials

The first problem you are likely to encounter is what to put in the title field. Most manuscripts do not have a title page as such. Some have a 'caption title', at the beginning of the first page; others just launch straight into the text. If you have a manuscript which consists of a single, easily identifiable work, such as a fifteenth-century Book of Hours, or a copy of the Anglo-Saxon Chronicle, you can supply what AACR calls a 'uniform title' for the whole manuscript quite easily. If, on the other hand, the manuscript you are cataloguing consists of a number of different works bound into one volume, you will have to do each one separately and possibly also make an extra record for the volume as a whole, linking all the records together in some way which shows the relationship between them. If you are cataloguing a letter or someone's diary, you will have to supply a descriptive title, which is likely to be rather vaguer than you would wish, for example:

Title   [Letter from Cynthia Lustgirdle to Amanda Droope, dated 10 May 1926]

This may be as specific as you can make the title without going into exhaustive detail (if you must, you could add a note about the content of the document). It is not going to help Minerva Sherlock, a researcher who is looking through the 200 or so letters which Cynthia wrote in May 1926 to find the one which contains vital information about the Gargoyle Press edition of *Dentures of Desire*. If you have added a note about the subject of the letter which contains the relevant keywords ('dentures' or 'gargoyle' for example) and notes are indexed in your catalogue, then she could find the right letter by doing a combined search for [letter] and [dentures or powderpuff]. Of course, when you are cataloguing 200 or so letters with almost identical bibliographic characteristics, it is quite difficult to pick out the significant pieces of information which ought to be included in the catalogue record, especially as Timothy Holmes at the next table is not interested at all in things which would have Minerva screaming with joy and reaching for her notebook, but is interested in references to Cynthia's cat because he is writing a book on authors and their cats.[5]

The crucial point to remember when cataloguing archives, if you do not want to spend your entire career creating an exhaustive index to the Lustgirdle letters (or similar), is that an archivist who wishes to remain relatively sane considers the collection to be the basic unit of information rather than the individual items within it. So, if you had the job of cataloguing the Lustgirdle archive you would begin by creating a *collection-level* description, with an overview of what the archive contains, who it is about, whether it is still being added to, what the conditions of access are, and so on. Next, you might wish to create intermediate-level records for different categories of material: a record with details of the diaries deposited in the collection, another about the letters. Then you might add another layer of records, to enable users of the archive to narrow their search within the broad categories: a single diary, or a box of letters. Finally, you could add records referring to individual items: one letter, or even a single entry in a diary. You would not necessarily want to go through the archive making records for each individual item; instead you would pick out the ones which seem most significant to you. You can always add extra records in the future if a researcher draws your attention to something important which does not have an individual record, and in the meantime the higher-level records give a good overall view of what is in the collection and where to find it.

Life has recently become a lot easier for archives cataloguers with the advent of a number of cataloguing standards designed specifically for archival materials. The General International Standard Archival Description, or ISAD(G) (1994), provides rules for the type of multi-level description outlined above. The International Standard Archival Authority Record for Corporate Bodies, Persons and Families (ISAAR) (1996) and the National Council on Archives' *Rules for the Construction of Personal, Place and Corporate Names* (NCA Rules, 1997) together provide a framework for creating access points and developing authority files. Finally, the standard for Encoded Archival Description (EAD) developed by the Library of

Congress offers a standardised way of formatting the record. Together, these may be used in place of the more familiar general library standards (AACR/MARC) to enable archivists to produce records which are consistent and may be exchanged between different organisations or contributed to union catalogues such as the Scottish Archive Network (SCAN).

Early printed books

"William Caxton! For all your printing needs! Come to William Caxton…"

Moveable-type printing began in Europe in the mid-fifteenth century. Books produced during the first fifty years after this are sometimes referred to as *incunabula* or *incunables*. The very first printed books were produced in the same basic format as manuscripts, with no title page. Some had hand-illuminated capitals, with only the main body of the text being printed; the name of the printer, the address of his place of business and (usually) the date when the book was printed appeared at the end of the text in the colophon. Figures 8.9 and 8.10 provide an example: the first page and colophon of Pietro de Crescenzi's *Ruralia commoda*, published in Augsburg in 1471. The capital on the first page is hand-illuminated in red.

Figure 8.9 First page of *Ruralia commoda*, with hand-illuminated capital

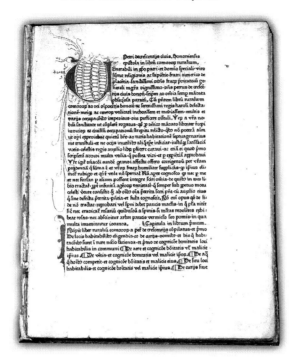

However, it was not long before printers were experimenting with new ways of presenting the bibliographic information about their texts and by the turn of the century (*c*.1500) most books had some form of title page, with the name of the author (if any) and the title of the book prominently displayed. Some also had the publication details in the place where you would expect to find them in a modern book, i.e. at the bottom of the title page: others continued to place this information in the colophon. The practice of putting information about the publisher in the colophon went out of fashion (at least, in Britain) in the seventeenth century, but some more modern texts, for example those from small presses associated with the Arts and Crafts movement (late nineteenth and early twentieth century) were also printed like this. So, if you are working on a book which does not seem to have any information about the publisher or printer, it is worth checking the back of the book to see if there is a colophon. In fact, if you are cataloguing a book for your library's special collections, it is worth checking the back of the book even if you think you have all the information you need, because some printers had the sneaky habit of putting brief details on the title page and then adding more information in a colophon. Others put false information on the title page to conceal their real identity. This was a well-known ruse in late eighteenth-century France, where controversial books which would not have been passed for publication by the censor were printed with the name of a non-existent printer allegedly doing business somewhere outside France (London and Amsterdam were favourite choices) on the title page – these are called fictitious imprints. You may not realise when you are cataloguing them that there is anything fishy about them, but if you are in the habit of checking a national or large academic library catalogue for bibliographic records to crib, you should find that their cataloguer has spotted the bogus publisher and put a note in about it. If you cannot find a record on anyone else's database to help, and you have reason to believe that the imprint is fictitious, try looking in relevant reference books such as E. Weller's *Die falschen und fingirten Druckorte* to see if the title is listed in there, or check directories of printers and publishers active at that time to see if the firm on your title page is listed; for early British publishers, this would normally mean checking Plomer's *Dictionaries of the printers and booksellers who were at work in England, Scotland and Ireland 1557–1775*. If you have checked everywhere you can think of and still not found any evidence that the information about the imprint on your title page is bogus, assume it is OK and put it into your catalogue record as it stands. After all, hunches can be wrong.

Figure 8.10 Colophon of *Ruralia commoda*, showing imprint

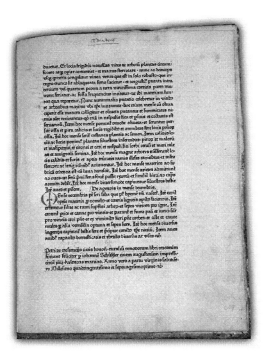

Something else to bear in mind, particularly when cataloguing eighteenth-century books, is the format of the book. Format, in this context, means whether a book is folio, quarto, octavo, duodecimo... (etc.). This does not refer to the size of the book, although format has an effect on size: it refers to the number of pages printed on one pass through the press. You can check this by looking at the bottom of each right-hand page; there will be a running sequence of guide numbers and/or letters to show the printers and binders which order the pages should appear in. These guide numbers are called signatures: the sequence for an octavo book (eight pages per pass through the press, 16 pages per sheet of paper if printed on both sides) would usually run A1 A2 A3 A4 A5, followed by three pages with no signatures, then B1 B2 B3 B4 B5 ... Sometimes asterisks are used instead of letters, e.g. *1 *2 *3 *4 *5 ... **1 **2 **3 **4 **5... [etc.]. It is important to check more than one sequence, because some of the smaller formats may have strange signatures; a duodecimo book (12 pages per pass through the press) may have a signature sequence which runs A1 A2 A3 A4 A5 ... B1 B2 B3 . C1 C2 C3 C4 C5 ... [etc.]. It is also important to check the main body of the text rather than the very beginning or the very end; sometimes the prefaces of a book would be printed separately to the main text. In these circumstances, checking the signatures for the prefaces could give you the wrong format.

Signatures are also used to work out the *fingerprints* of a document: these are points of comparison between different copies of a title which are used to establish whether the copies belong to the same edition – not the dirty marks left by a careless printer! The usual method is to record the letter from the main body of the text which appears immediately above the signature letter: this allows librarians and bibliographers to compare different copies of a work without having to put them physically side by side. It is not always possible to tell from the title page whether a given copy is a genuine new edition of a work or a reissue of the former edition with a new (or variant) title page; checking the fingerprints will give you this information, but not many libraries (even among those which otherwise devote a great deal of effort to their special collections) record fingerprints.

Format for early printed books is important because some publishers produced different sizes of the same text for different markets, rather in the way that modern publishers produce hardbacks, trade paperbacks and ordinary-sized (what the Americans call mass-market) paperbacks. The Foulis brothers of Glasgow, for example, would often produce two printings of the same edition of a book, one octavo size for the impoverished student and the middle classes and a quarto size 'large paper' edition for the more wealthy bookaholic. The large paper edition would be produced using the same text blocks as the octavo edition, but printed on higher quality paper with a larger margin around the text. The only certain way to tell the two editions apart is to look at the format; simply measuring the size doesn't always help, since a quarto copy which has been cut down a lot by the binder may not be very different in size from an octavo copy which has not. Look carefully at the gutter margins (the white space running down the middle of the book). If these are very wide and you know that the book you are cataloguing was produced in a large-paper format, it is quite likely that the copy you have is large-paper. Ideally, you should compare it with an ordinary-sized copy to make sure, but this is not usually practical unless you are lucky enough to have two copies, one in each format.

If you are cataloguing early printed books, the best way to do it is to follow an approved standard for these materials, either the Library of Congress' *Descriptive Cataloging of Rare Books* (DCRB, available online) or ISBD(A), the international standard for the bibliographic description of antiquarian books. AACR also has additional rules for cataloguing early printed materials.

Finally, remember that there is a purpose to all these tedious bibliographic details you are wearing your fingers out recording. Before 1830, when the Victorians invented mechanical presses, all printing was done in hand presses and all other aspects of book production (typesetting, collation, binding...) were done by hand. We are used to automated book production and uniformity between different copies of the same title; the amount of variation was much greater in hand-produced books. So even though your copy of *The first booke of cattel* is not unique in the same way as the Lindisfarne Gospels, it is still worth spending extra time over.

Graphic materials: pictures, postcards, book illustrations...

We have already considered the basic problems of cataloguing these types of material in Chapter 5. What more do you need to know? Well, if you are working in an ordinary sort of library on a non-research collection, the answer is not a lot.

If, on the other hand, you are working on a catalogue of the National Art Library's pictures, or Much Gossip's postcard collection which in turn is part of their local history collection, it is possible that the users of your catalogue will be interested in more than just what the thing is (the descriptive cataloguing) and what it represents (the subject access). In fact, like the researchers we met earlier, they are likely to want to know what techniques were used to produce the things you are cataloguing, and in extreme cases what materials were used as well. It is quite likely that you will encounter Timothy again here, looking for illustrations suitable for his book on literary cats; his publisher will only accept black and white images, so he will want some way of separating them out from the colour ones. You may also encounter historians who are interested in the development of a particular printing or painting technique. Even book cataloguers are not safe from these people; some of them do research on book illustrations and want to know (ideally from the catalogue record, so they don't have to go through all the books on the shelf) which books have lithographs in them and which have hand-coloured woodcuts.

The Library of Congress has produced a thesaurus of terms for graphic materials (1986; also available online) along the same lines as the ACRL's thesauri for rare book terms. This is really intended for cataloguing collections of pictures, prints, photographs and postcards, but could also be used for book illustrations. For example, let us suppose that the Cursed Powderpuff edition of *Dentures of Desire* has a hand-coloured woodcut as its frontispiece:

[Bibliographic description]

Title	Dentures of desire
Author, etc.	Cynthia Lustgirdle; illustrated by William Rembrandt Robinson
Publication	London: Cursed Powderpuff Press, 2003
Series	Pinnacles of passion
Format	Text
Size/extent	452 p., 23 cm
Illustrations	1 coloured plate (frontispiece; hand-coloured woodcut)
Language	English
ISBN	132456257123X
Printer	Printed by Joseph Bloggs
Editions	First published in 1926 by the Gargoyle Press; this edition is limited to 250 copies
Local note	Copy no. 3
Inscriptions etc.	Signed by the author; presented to the library by Gillian Smith in memory of her mother Elizabeth Smith (aka Cynthia Lustgirdle) – RE/U-1
Binding	Publisher's original paper binding – RE/U-1

[Access points]

Author	Lustgirdle, Cynthia
Title	Dentures of desire

Series	Pinnacles of passion
Subject	Dentists (Fiction)
	Romantic fiction
Illustrator	Robinson, William Rembrandt
Publisher	Cursed Powderpuff Press
Previous owner	Smith, Gillian
Binding	Publishers' paper bindings (Binding) – England – London – 21st century – rbbin – RE/U-1
Provenance	Authors' autographs (Provenance) – Great Britain – 21st century – rbprov – RE/U-1
Publishing	Limitation statements (Publishing) – England – London – 21st century – rbpub
GMD[6]	Woodcuts – Coloured – England – London – 21st century – gmgpc

This allows you to provide an index for different types of graphic material, so that researchers interested exclusively in woodcuts do not have to waste their time looking at a lot of lithographs. Providing additional access points is especially useful if you have a large collection of illustrated books; if you have collections of prints, photos or postcards you can always file the different kinds in different places – lithographs in one box, mezzotints in another, and so on – but this is not usually practical for books; most library users prefer to have these grouped by author and/or subject (and what would you do with a book which had more than one type of illustration?).

Telling styles of printing
apart: "I think this one's
from the 'bad' school of
printing."

Problems you are likely to encounter include:

1. *What the **** is it?* It's not always easy even for an expert to tell different kinds of printing technique apart. After five years working as a rare books cataloguer, I can usually tell the difference between aquatints and coloured lithographs: I am not so good at recognising mezzotints, possibly because I haven't seen many examples of them. If you are really not sure what something is, there are no clues in the document itself to help and you don't have a friendly neighbourhood expert who can tell you, it is better to leave the extra information out of the record than guess and get it wrong.

2. *How important is it?* If you are working on a big collection of national importance, you will want to put every possible detail about the item you are cataloguing into the record. If you are working on a non-research collection you may not want to put any of these extra details in. If you are somewhere in between, and want to restrict the extra details to significant and/or unusual items, you need to find out what's important and what isn't, also what is normal and what isn't, before you can make judgements about what to put in and what to leave out.

3. *Should I include a digital image on the database?* The answer to this question depends partly on how much storage capacity you have on your system (image files are big!) and partly on copyright. If the item you are cataloguing is out of copyright or your organisation is the copyright holder and is willing to allow a digital image to be added to the catalogue record, there is no problem. If not, you will need to ask permission of the copyright holder and possibly pay a fee for the right to reproduce it digitally – a time-consuming and potentially expensive process.

Children's books and related materials

'Rude books are definitely not allowed in the school library,' said Miss Rogers severely. 'Parents would want to borrow them, and they would never be on the shelves.'

Margaret Mahy, *A Villain's Night Out*

Children's librarians have a slight image problem: many people assume that children's librarianship is easy because, well, children's books are easier to read than grown-up ones. Cataloguers of children's books have a similar problem: many people, including some who should know better, assume that cataloguing children's books is easy compared to cataloguing books intended for adults. Actually, like any other kind of cataloguing, it can be as easy or as difficult as you wish to make it and has several specific issues which are not really as important in 'adult' cataloguing.

There are two basic types of children's collection:

1. Collections intended for use by children – found in public and school libraries, featuring a wide range of fiction and non-fiction and usually including audio books and videos. Some public libraries now provide a separate 'young adult' collection for teenagers in addition to their children's collection.

2. Collections intended for researchers and teachers – collections for researchers are usually found in national or academic libraries; collections for teachers are found in teacher training establishments and the schools department of public library services and may include teaching aids ('big books', filmstrips, collections of slides, etc.) and curriculum documents as well as children's fiction and non-fiction.

The two different types of collection have slightly different aims. A collection intended for use by children (and their parents) will have the aim of supporting the child's development and providing materials which are both useful (for cognitive, social and educational development) and enjoyable for the child to use. In the UK at this moment, that means supporting the National Curriculum's objectives, which includes teaching children how to use finding aids such as indexes, encyclopaedias, computer databases... and library catalogues. The collection will have to provide appropriate materials for children aged from 0 to 18; it should also provide for children with special needs, including for example blind and partially sighted children and any whose first language is not English. The librarians selecting, arranging and cataloguing the collection will also need to be aware of controversial documents which may cause offence to some users of the collection. A research collection, on the other hand, is intended to be used by adults, so what is considered important for cataloguing purposes will vary according to the overall purpose of the collection. A collection for the use of trainee teachers, for example, may not be divided up according to age range in order to force students to form their own judgements about whether a particular book (tape, video...) is suitable for the group or class they are working with on teaching practice. A 'special ' collection of children's books, on the other hand, may be catalogued to the Rolls-Royce standard for the benefit of researchers in children's literature and social history; they will probably want to know that *this* is the book which caused all the fuss when it won the Carnegie medal in 2004, and where to find the key reviews and newspaper articles about it, also who illustrated it, who designed the bookjacket... in short, the same kind of things which you would have to add to the record for an early printed book.

Fifty years ago, it would have been unheard of to spend time and effort on creating detailed catalogue records for children's books in order to make them more easily retrievable by researchers. Most academics were involved in serious research on Important and Significant Subjects. It is only really within the last thirty years or so that social and literary historians have realised that children's literature is a rich source of information about the past. If the art of other cultures and previous generations holds up a mirror to life in their society, then children's literature shows them as they would like to be. Even something as simple as an early nineteenth-century child's ABC can be a goldmine: it shows everyday objects which an average child would have been familiar with, which are not necessarily the same as the everyday objects in a modern ABC.

The following are the key issues you will need to think about when working with books and other resources intended for children:

1. *Censorship*. If a book in the children's library contains material likely to cause offence to some library users, should there be a note in the catalogue record or some other indication that it is controversial (a sticker on the book, for example)? Of course, human nature being what it is, this may simply serve to draw attention to the controversial book and increase the number of people who read it...

2. *Intended audience*. Should things in the children's collection be divided up according to the age range they are intended for? If so, are they going to be identified as being for a particular age range in the catalogue or just given colour-coded labels and/or shelved in different areas of the library?

3. *Format* – for example, pop-up or lift-the-flap books for preschool children. This could be important in both types of library; some children love this kind of interactive book, and some researchers are fascinated by paper engineering.

4. *Subject access*. If you are providing subject headings or keywords in the catalogue record and your catalogue also

has records for documents *not* intended for children, you will need some way of distinguishing between records for children's materials and records for everything else, so that people can select adult or children's books on the subject they are interested in as appropriate. The Library of Congress provides a list of children's subject headings which uses simpler language for some (though not all) subjects in order to make them more accessible to children; an alternative approach would be to use the same heading that would be used for an adult book on the same subject, but add the subdivision 'Juvenile literature' or 'Juvenile fiction' to it. This would have the advantage of putting adult and children's books next to each other in the subject index.

5. *Genre headings and subject access to fiction.* Most public libraries do not provide this, as being too time-consuming. However, it can be helpful to have subject information about fiction in the catalogue, especially if you have a large collection. The School of Education library at Reading does add subject headings to records for children's fiction, which once helped me find a book for a student who wanted to read her class a story about an animal which lived in a cold place to support the topic they were studying.[7] Children who have enjoyed reading a book will look for other ones like it, either by the same author or in a similar style by a different author. Ask any children's librarian how many times he or she has been asked for another book 'just like Harry Potter' if you don't believe me.

"I can't help but notice that you've classified 'Winnie the Pooh' under 'Nobody Knows (Tiddley Pom)'"

Subject headings are a particular bone of contention in cataloguing children's collections, as we have seen. Casting our minds back to Chapter 2 (if you can remember that far back!) we remember that the Much Gossip public library, with only one cataloguer single-handedly attempting to hold back the backlog, decided to stop providing subject headings for children's resources. This is quite a common time-saving wheeze in libraries with understaffed cataloguing departments; either the quality of the records is downgraded or the job of creating them is passed to a library assistant rather than a professional cataloguer. Sometimes it is the only possible solution to the problem of increasing cataloguing throughput and/or lowering costs, but it should be undertaken reluctantly. Children's libraries are used by people too! In other words, the people who use these collections deserve our best efforts to serve them, just as users of other library collections do. Researchers into children's literature are just as scholarly and passionate about their subject as researchers into other, 'grown-up' subjects are, and children who use school and public libraries need accurate, comprehensive catalogues to tell them what's available if they are to grow up into Ideal Library Users, confident in performing all but the most complicated literature searches for themselves. How are they to develop expertise in subject searching if the library catalogue does not have anything except the classmark to show what a particular book is about? Besides, cataloguing children's books is fun – but perhaps you'd better not make too much of this when you are trying to talk the boss out of taking your children's cataloguing away from you and giving it to someone else...

Electronic resources

This term covers a multitude of formats, ranging from full-text documents held on your own intranet through CD-Roms, floppy disks and CD-Is to remote websites not maintained by your organisation. Cataloguing electronic resources which are contained in a physical object like a CD-Rom is relatively straightforward: you simply have to decide whether it is a finite resource or a continuing one. Cataloguing websites, especially ones not maintained by your own organisation, is not quite so easy, because you are cataloguing a moving target. Websites are continually being remodelled, expanded, moved and discontinued, so maintaining an accurate record of a resource under these circumstances can be difficult. This is where it is helpful to have metadata embedded in the actual electronic document: when the document is updated, the metadata will be changed as well. However, if you are creating a record on your own database for something which is available over the Internet but is not in your control, the catalogue record is not linked to the document in the same way and you will have to work out some way of checking regularly to see if it is still there.

Some libraries have got around this problem by not cataloguing remote electronic resources unless they pay a subscription for access. The advantage of this approach is that you will know when your subscription ceases (whether because the service is discontinued or because you can't afford it) and so will be alerted to the fact that the catalogue needs to be amended. The disadvantage is that your users may be unaware of equally useful free resources because you have not added them to the catalogue. A good compromise here would be to provide a list of useful resources on your own library website, which could be checked regularly for broken links. This job is often done by the reference staff, who then notify the cataloguers of any changes needed.

Another strategy you may wish to try (for information you can't live without) is contacting the owner of the website you are interested in and asking permission to copy it for your own library. The copy might be an electronic copy or a printout; if the original mysteriously vanishes from cyberspace overnight, at least you would still have the copy.

For full-text electronic documents, it may be worthwhile adding an embedded index to the document. This uses our old friend XML to code significant words and concepts in an electronic document. It is even more labour-intensive than ordinary cataloguing, but if you are the knowledge manager for your organisation it may be worth doing for particularly significant documents.

So, to sum up:

1. *Is it worth cataloguing?* Don't try to catalogue the whole of the Internet – life is too short, and quite a lot of what's

out there is, frankly, rubbish. Concentrate on high-quality sites providing reliable information which is relevant to your users' needs.

2. *Less is more...* for once. In other words, do not put too much detail in the records for remote electronic resources. You want your catalogue to be as accurate as possible; if you get carried away and add lots of extra information to the record, it just makes more things you have to check. Describe the website (or whatever) as concisely as possible, given that the description has to provide enough information to the catalogue users to enable them to decide whether or not the resource is going to be useful to them.

3. *Is it still there?* Set up a routine for checking that the online resources you have catalogued are still functional. You may want to check once a week, once a month or once every three months or so, depending on how much the site is used and how likely it is to disappear. The routine check could be done automatically by the system (if your system is clever enough) or by a library assistant (if you have one). It is probably not worth setting up a daily check; if you have online resources which are used that much, your colleagues and/or the library users will tell you all about it (probably at great length) the moment there is a problem.

Notes

1. There are also two bookplates inside the book, showing that it subsequently belonged to J.R. McCulloch and Samuel, Baron Overstone; this is somewhat less exciting.

2. In our dreams...

3. I have used the code for Reading University Library, as being the one I am most familiar with. Needless to say, there is no copy of *Dentures of Desire* at Reading, with or without an author's autograph!

4. A nice clear inscription – they are not all as easy to read as that one!

5. On the other hand, if you make things too easy for Timothy, it will take away the thrill of the chase!

6. Graphic material designation (well, that's what the Library of Congress calls it).

7. The following week she came back wanting a story about an animal which lived somewhere hot and we couldn't find one. You win some, you lose some...

Appendix
Resources for cataloguers

In this appendix I have attempted to give a representative list of resources (online and printed) which I have found helpful in the course of my work. I have not listed websites and books dealing with specific subjects other than cataloguing and thesauri or thesaurus construction, although I have included a reference to the BUBL subject tree, which provides links to subject-specific web resources. I have tried to avoid providing multiple references to the same website, except in the case of the Library of Congress, where there is so much information freely available on such a wide range of subjects that simply providing the location of the homepage seemed inadequate.

National library websites

British Library: *http://www.bl.uk/*

IFLANET: web accessible national and major libraries [online]. Available at: *http://ifla.org/II/natlibs.htm*

Library of Congress: *http://www.loc.gov/*

National Library of Australia: *http://www.nla.gov.au/*

National Library of Canada: *http://www.amicus.nlc-bnc.ca/*

Gateways and general reference sources

Dmoz open directory project: Reference: Libraries: Library and Information Science: Technical Services: Cataloguing. Available at: *http://dmoz.org/Reference/Libraries/Library _and_Information_Science/Technical_Services/Cataloguing*

The Librarians' Index to the Internet. Available at: *http:// lii.org/*

Xrefer. Available at: *http://www.xrefer.com/*

International standards

Anglo-American Cataloguing Rules, 2nd edn, 2002 revision. Ottawa: Canadian Library Association.

British Library. *UKMARC Manual* [online]. Available at: *http://www.bl.uk/services/bibliographic/marc/marcman.html*

Dublin Core Metadata Element Set, Version 1.1: Reference Description [online]. Available at: *http://dublincore.org/ documents/dces/*

Harold, E.R. (2002). *XML in a Nutshell*, 2nd edn. Sebastopol, CA: O'Reilly.

International Council on Archives (1994) *ISAD(G): General International Standard Archival Description.* Ottawa: International Council on Archives.

International Council on Archives. (1996) *ISAAR (CPF): International Standard Archival Authority Record for Corporate Bodies, Persons and Families.* Ottawa: International Council on Archives.

International Federation of Library Associations and Institutions. *ISBD(G): General International Standard*

Bibliographic Description, revised edn. Available online at: *http://www.ifla.org/VII/s13/pubs/isbdg.htm*

Library of Congress. *Encoded Archival Description* (EAD) [online]. Available at: *http://www.loc.gov/ead/*

Library of Congress. *MARC Standards* [online]. Available at: *http://www.loc.gov/marc/*

National Council on Archives (1997) *Rules for the Construction of Personal, Place and Corporate Names.* London: National Council on Archives.

ONIX International Release 1.2.1 [online]. Available for download as a PDF file at: *http://www.editeur.org/onixfiles1.2.1/onixfiles.html*

Research Support Libraries Programme (2000) *RSLP Collection Description: Collection Description Schema* [online]. Available at: *http://www.ukoln.ac.uk/metadata/rslp/schema/*

Tennant, R. (ed.) (2002) *XML in Libraries.* New York: Neal-Schuman.

XML Standards Reference [online]. Available at: *http://www.webreference.com/xml/reference/standards.html*

Introductions to AACR/MARC

Catskill Interactive Multimedia Package: Version 3 [CD-Rom] (2003). Available in the UK from: Facet Publishing. ISBN 185604503X.

Bowman, J.H. (2003) *Essential Cataloguing.* London: Facet Publishing.

Fritz, D.A. (1998) *Cataloging with AACR2R and USMARC for Books, Computer Files, Serials, Sound Recordings,*

Videorecordings. Chicago and London: American Library Association.

Authority control

Ballard, T. *Typographical Errors in Library Databases* [online]. Available at: *http://faculty.quinnipiac.edu/libraries/tballard/typoscomplete.html*

The Catholic Encyclopedia [online]. Available at: *http://www.newadvent.org/cathen/* (good source for verifying ancient and mediaeval names).

Getty Research Institute. *Vocabulary Databases* [online]. Available at: *http://www.getty.edu/research/tools/vocabulary/* (includes *Art and Architecture Thesaurus (AAT)*, *Thesaurus of Geographical Names (TGN)* and *Union List of Artists' Names (ULAN)*).

HURIDOCS. *How to Record the Names of Persons* [pdf file online]. Available from: *http://www.huridocs.org/popnames.htm* (deals with contemporary names only).

Library of Congress. *Authorities* [online]. Available at: *http://authorities.loc.gov/*

Thesaurus construction

Aitchison, J., Gilchrist, A. and Bawden, D. (2000) *Thesaurus Construction and Use: A Practical Manual*, 4th edn. London: Aslib.

British Standards Institution (1987) *Guide to Establishment and Development of Monolingual Thesauri.* London: British Standards Institution (BS 5723: 1987) (ISO 2788: 1986).

Subject and genre thesauri

BUBL LINK: Browse LINK by Subject [online]. Available at: *http://bubl.ac.uk/link/subjects/*

Library of Congress. *Thesauri: Services and Other Resources* [online] Available at: *http://www.loc.gov/library/libarch-thesauri.html*

Taves, B., Hoffman, J. and Lund, K. (1998) *The Moving Image Genre-Form Guide* [online]. Available at: *http://lcweb.loc.gov/rr/mopic/migintro.html*

Foreign languages

ALA-LC Romanization Tables [online]. Available at: *http://lcweb.loc.gov/catdir/cpso/roman.html*

Dictsearch. Available at: *http://www.foreignword.com/Tools/dictsrch.htm*

Special collections cataloguing

Association of College and Research Libraries and American Library Association (1986) *Printing and Publishing Evidence: Thesauri for Use in Rare Book and Special*

Collections Cataloguing. Chicago: Association of College and Research Libraries. Available online at: *http://www.ala.org/ACRL/.*

Association of College and Research Libraries and American Library Association (1988) *Binding Terms: A Thesaurus for Use in Rare Book and Special Collections Cataloguing.* Chicago: Association of College and Research Libraries. Available online at: *http://www.ala.org/ACRL/.*

Association of College and Research Libraries and American Library Association (1988) *Provenance Evidence: Thesaurus for Use in Rare Books and Special Collections Cataloguing.* Chicago: Association of College and Research Libraries. Available online at: *http://www.ala.org/ACRL/.*

Association of College and Research Libraries and American Library Association (1990) *Paper Terms: A Thesaurus for Use in Rare Book and Special Collections Cataloguing.* Chicago: Association of College and Research Libraries. Available online at: *http://www.ala.org/ACRL/.*

Association of College and Research Libraries and American Library Association (1990) *Type Evidence: A Thesaurus for Use in Rare Book and Special Collections Cataloguing.* Chicago: Association of College and Research Libraries. Available online at: *http://www.ala.org/ACRL/.*

Bibliographic Standards Committee. *Latin Place Names* [online]. Available at: *http://www.lib.byu.edu/~catalog/people/rlm/latin/names.html*

Library Association Rare Books Group (1997) *Guidelines for the Cataloguing of Rare Books.* London: Library Association Rare Books Group.

Library of Congress. *Descriptive Cataloging of Rare Books*, 2nd edn [online]. Available at: *http://www.tlcdelivers.com/ tlc/crs/rare0170.htm*

Library of Congress. *Thesaurus for Graphic Materials II: Genre and Physical Characteristic Headings*. Washington, DC: Library of Congress. Cataloguing Distribution Service. Available online at: *http://www.loc.gov/rr/print/tgm2/*.

Plomer, H.R. et al. (1977) *Dictionaries of the Printers and Booksellers Who Were at Work in England, Scotland and Ireland 1557–1775*. Ilkley: The Bibliographical Society (gives biographical details and street addresses, where known, for each person listed, together with dates when they were active in their profession; invaluable source of dates for distinguishing between printers and publishers with the same name).

Victoria and Albert Museum (1962) *Early Printers' Marks*. London: HMSO.

Bibliography

Aitchison, J., Gilchrist, A. and Bawden, D. (2000) *Thesaurus Construction and Use: A Practical Manual*, 4th edn. London: Aslib.

Bowman, J.H. (2003) *Essential Cataloguing*. London: Facet Publishing.

Bridge, N. (2003) 'Verifying personal names on the Web', *The Indexer*, 23(3): 149–56.

Chapman, Anne (2002) 'Demystifying metadata', *Catalogue & Index*, 146: 1–6.

Coates, E.J. (1988) *Subject Catalogues: Headings and Structure*. London: Library Association.

Cutter, C.A. and US Office of Education (1971). *Public Libraries in the United States of America: Their History, Condition and Management*. Totowa, NJ: Rowman & Littlefield.

Danskin, A. (2001) 'ONIX international: how better product information sells more books: report of BIC seminar 14 November 2000', *Catalogue & Index*, 139: 6–7.

Fiander, D.J. (2001) 'Applying XML to the bibliographic description', *Cataloging and Classification Quarterly*, 33 (2): 17–28.

Foskett, A.C. (1982) *The Subject Approach to Information*, 4th edn. London: Clive Bingley.

Fritz, D.A. (1998) *Cataloging with AACR2R and USMARC for Books, Computer Files, Serials, Sound Recordings, Videorecordings*. Chicago and London: American Library Association.

Hoerman, H.L. (2002) 'Why does everybody hate cataloging?', *Cataloging and Classification Quarterly*, 34 (1): 31–41.

International Federation of Library Associations and Institutions (1998) *Functional Requirements for Bibliographic Records: Final Report*. Available online at: *http://www.ifla.org/VII/s13/frbr/frbr.htm*

Marcella, R., Robson, H. and Brown, A.J.E. (2003) 'Cataloguing practice in archive collections in the United Kingdom', *Catalogue & Index*, 148: 1–5.

Morris, D.E. (1992) 'Staff time and costs for cataloging', *Library Resources and Technical Services*, 36 (1): 79–95.

Morris, D.E. and Wool, G. (1999) 'Cataloging: librarianship's best bargain', *Library Journal*, 15 June: 44–6.

Rowley, J.E. and Farrow, J. (2000) *Organizing Knowledge: An Introduction to Managing Access to Information*. Aldershot: Gower.

Ryan, F. (1999) 'European Bank for Reconstruction and Development', in S. Simmons (ed.), *Information Insights: Case Studies in Information Management*. London: Aslib, pp. 92–5.

Tennant, R. (2002) 'MARC must die', *Library Journal* [online], 15 October. Available from: *http://libraryjournal .reviewsnews.com/index.asp?layout=article&articleid= CA250046&publication=libraryjournal*

Van Veen, T. (2002) 'Searching and retrieving XML records via the Web', in R. Tennant (ed.), *XML in Libraries*. New York: Neal-Schuman, pp. 17–30.

Webb, S.P. (1998) *Knowledge Management: Linchpin of Change*. London: Aslib.

Index

AACR, 6, 71–5, 88, 100, 123–4, 168, 195, 204
  chief source of information, 119–21
  main entry, 72–4, 129–30
  rule of three, 73–4
  selection of access points, 72
Abstracts, 31, 137
Accents, 170
Access points, 20, 25–30, 72
  advanced, 27–9
  basic, 27
  consistency in, 99–105
  physical characteristics of document, 186–8, 207
  Rolls-Royce, 29–30, 182
Analytical cataloguing – *see* Granularity
Anglo-American Cataloguing Rules – *see* AACR
Anglo-American spelling differences, 98–9
Archives, 24, 195–8
Armorial bindings, 180–1
Author, problems in identifying, 122–3, 129–30, 131–2
Authority control, 65, 97–105
  skills needed, 47

Babylonian demon bowls, 31, 132

Bacco in Toscana, 179–81
Backlogs, 54–5
Benefits of cataloguing, 15–17
Biblia Hebraica, 160–1, 168
Bibliographic description, 7, 20–5, 69, 72, 121–5
  advanced, 22–3
  basic, 21–2
  conflicting information, 119
  Rolls-Royce, 23–5, 182
  skills needed, 44–5
Boudoirs of Passion, 73–4
Bowman, J.H., 13–14

Callimachus, 5
Canadian official publications, 167–8
Caption title, 195
Card catalogues, 9, 82
Cataloguing:
  history, 5–6
  importance of, 3–5, 9
  policy, 33–4
  speeds, 48–51
  staff, 47–8
CD-Roms, 133, 215
Censorship, 212
Chief source of information, 119–21
Children's collections, 209–15
  censorship, 212

formats, 212
key issues, 212–13
Chinese (Mandarin), 23, 158,
159, 160
Chinese, cultural differences, 171
Coates, E.J., 28
Coding standards – *see* MARC,
XML
Collection Description, 79–82, 86
Collection-level records, 126,
196–7
Collective title, 121, 122
Colophon, 198–200
Command-driven programs, 62
Computer catalogues, 9, 17
Computer systems:
key questions, 58–9, 63–5
selection of, 59–60, 63–6
Computerised translation
programs, 171
Computers as cataloguers,
limitations of, 14
Contents tables, 31, 126
Context of documents, 185
Continuing resources, 110–11
Controlled subject vocabulary,
37, 39, 91–6, 143, 145
Controversial literature, 39–40
Copyright, 31
Copy-specific details, 188–9
Costs of cataloguing, 14–17
Cross-references, 65
Cultural differences 171
Cutter, C.A., 5–6

Data attributes, Collection
Description, 80–1
Data elements:
DC, 75–6

ISBD, 69–70
MARC, 83–4
ONIX, 78
Database programs, 61
Dates, problems with, 124,
189–94
DC – *see* Dublin Core
DCRB, 204
Degrees of Fear, 176–8
Demon bowls, 31, 132
Dentures of Desire, 22–5, 27,
29–30, 32, 70–1, 76, 78, 84,
86–7, 138, 187–8, 205–7;
see also Lustgirdle archive
Descriptive Cataloguing of Rare
Books, 204
Descriptive cataloguing – *see*
Bibliographic description
Dictionaries, 171
Dictionary catalogues, 9
Digital images, 31, 85–6, 181,
209
Distinctive title, 122
Document, definition of, xi
Drum & IBC Guide, 113–18
Dublin Core, 6, 75, 86
DVDs, 120, 124, 130–1, 167

EAD, 197–8
Early printed books, 29, 31,
123–4, 198–204
fingerprints, 202–3
formats, 201–2
large paper editions, 203–4
printers and publishers,
199–201
signatures, 202–3
Edition, 123
Electronic resources, 133, 215–17

Embedded indexes, 137, 216
Embedded metadata, 75–7, 88, 215
Encoded Archival Description, 197–8
English, relationships with other languages, 156–7
Enhancements, 20, 30–2, 85–6, 182, 209
Extended character set, 170
Extensible Markup Language – see XML

Fascicules, 127–8
Fiander, David J., 89
Fiction, assigning subject headings to, 150–2, 213
Fictitious imprints, 200–1
Films, 120, 130–1, 167
Fingerprints, 202–3
Finite resources, 110, 119–21
Formats:
    children's collections, 212
    definitions of, 109–11
    early printed books, 201–2
    key questions, 112–13
Forms, 62
Foskett, A.C., 4–5
French revolutionary calendar, 193–4
Fritz, D.A., 66

General International Standard Archival Description – see ISAD(G)
Genre headings, 28–9, 150–2, 213
German, 156

Global editing, 104
Grammar (foreign languages), 171–2
Granularity, 125–6
Graphic materials, 131–2, 204–9
Greek, 157, 162

Hebrew, 158, 159, 160–1
Hierarchical relationships between records, 89–90
Hoerman, H.L., 19, 43, 47
Hymns and Moral Songs, 192–3, 194
Hyperlinks, 26
Hypertext mark-up languages, 85

IFLA, 69
Illustrations, 190–1, 204–9
Inconsistent headings, strategies for dealing with, 105
Incunabula, 198–9
Indexes, 25
Indexing, 8, 137, 216
Indo-European languages, 156
Information management, definition of, x–xi
Inscriptions in documents, 191
Institute for Dental History (fictional), 140–1
Integrated library systems, 61
Integrating resources, 111
International Federation of Library Associations and Institutions – see IFLA
International Standard Archival Authority Record for Corporate Bodies, Persons and Families – see ISAAR

International Standard for
    Bibliographic Description –
    see ISBD
International standards, 15–16,
    67–8
Iowa State University Library,
    14–15, 50–1
ISAAR, 197
ISAD(G), 197
ISBD, 6, 23, 68–71, 168
ISBD(A), 71, 204
ISBD(G), 69
ISBN, 70, 112, 125
ISSN, 70, 112

Keywords, 26–7
KM:
    creating thesauri for, 93
    definition of, x–xi
Knowledge management – *see*
    KM

Languages:
    identification of, 158–9
    most likely to encounter,
        154–5
    relationships between, 155–8
Large paper editions, 203–4
Latin, 157, 172
LCSH, 39, 91–2, 104, 145,
    150–1
    children's subject headings,
        213
    difficulties with LCSH, 39
    free-floating subheadings, 92
    subheadings, 91–2
Library of Congress subject
    headings – *see* LCSH
Library of Congress, DCRB, 204

Limited editions, 176–8
Linguistics, 172
Lithographs, 190, 205
Loose-leaf files, 111
Lotus Notes, 61
Lustgirdle archive, 81–2, 196–7;
    see also Dentures of Desire

Machine-Readable Cataloguing –
    see MARC
Main entry, 72–4
Manuscript cataloguing,
    background information for,
        184–5
Manuscripts, 29, 195–8
Maps, 20, 129
MARC, 79, 80–5, 88–90
Material-specific data, 70
Medical Subject Headings, 93
Mental maps, 94–5
Menu-driven programs, 62
Metadata, 75–7, 88, 215
    definition of, xi–xii
Microsoft Access, 61, 65
Monographs, 109, 110
Morris, D.E., 14–15, 50–1
Much Gossip public library,
    34–6, 51–2, 125–6, 132,
    140, 205
Multi-disciplinary subjects, 28
Multilingual documents, 167–9
Multimedia resource centres, 110
Music, printed, 128

Name headings, 26–30, 100–4
    consolidation of, 8
    foreign and mediaeval, 75
    strategies for establishing,
        100–1

National Council on Archives
Rules (UK), 210
National Curriculum (UK), 210
NCA Rules, 197
Non-controlled subject
vocabulary, 38–9, 96–7,
138–9, 142–3
Non-European languages, 156,
157–8
Non-print materials, 30
Non-Roman writing systems,
159, 160–3

Objectivity, 37, 39–40
Objects, 132
ONIX, 77–9, 86, 87

Paintings – *see* Graphic materials
Panizzi, Sir Anthony, 5
Parallel texts, 167
Plato's Mistake, 146–7
Postcards – *see* Graphic materials
Printed documents, 119–20,
127–8
Prints – *see* Graphic materials
Problem documents, 54
*Protocols of the Wise Men of
Zion*, 39–40
Provenance, 176, 178, 181
Publication details, 123–4

Rare book cataloguing,
background information for,
184–5
Rare books, 24–5
bindings, 180–1, 183–4, 191–2
modern limited editions, 176–8
Recataloguing, 55
Recruitment difficulties, 13

Research Support Libraries
Programme (UK), 13, 80
Rich product information, 77
Romance languages, 156–7
Rule of three, 73–4
Ruralia commoda, 198–9, 201

Sentence case, 78–9
Serials, 109, 110–11, 112, 133–4
Series, 124–5
Signatures, 202–3
Signed bindings, 191–2
Skeletons, 132–3
Sound recordings, 120, 129–30,
170
Special collections, 175–6
Specialist thesauri, 93
Staffing ratios, 53
Standard number, 70, 125
Statement of responsibility, 23–4,
70
*Study of Volatile Precursors for
the Growth of Cadmium
Sulphide and Cadmium
Selenide...*, 143–5
Subject analysis, 137, 138–9
Subject cataloguing, 8, 37–40,
91–7, 137–52
broad subjects, 146
checklists, 141–2, 165–7
children's collections, 212–15
in foreign languages, 163–7
over-analysis of subject, 141
purpose of, 137
scientific subjects, 145–6,
163–4
skills needed, 45–6
verification of headings, 148–9
Subject headings, 26, 28–30

Subject terms, ONIX, 79
Subject trees, 94
Subject-specific vocabulary,
    148–9, 169–70
Supplements to journals, 113

Tale of Mrs Tittlemouse, 169
Targets, 34–6, 52–3, 56
Templates, 49, 87
Tennant, Roy, 88
Terms of availability 70
Thesauri, 91, 92–3, 143
Thesaurus construction, 93–6
Time management, 53–6
Title, 121–2
    main entry under title, 73–4
Title case, 78
Title page, development of,
    198–200
Toys, 132
Transliteration, 159, 160–3, 171
    of Chinese, 162
Truncation, 99
Twenty Years Behind the Drill,
    29, 139–41

Type ornaments, 180
Typographical errors, 97–8

Uniform title, 122, 195
University of Nowhereshire,
    81–2, 140, 150
User education, importance of,
    11–12
User interfaces, 62–3
Users' needs, 10–12

Videos, 120, 124, 130–1, 167
Virtual libraries, 61, 110
Virtues of a good catalogue, 8
Websites, 111, 133, 215–17
Wild card character, 99
Wspolczesni historycy Brytyjscy,
    164–5, 168–9

XML, 85–8, 90, 216

Yearbooks, 113

Z39.50 protocol, 80